THE TRUE STORY OF
GRACE O'MALLEY

✦

# IRELAND'S
## PIRATE QUEEN

ANNE CHAMBERS

MJF BOOKS
NEW YORK

Published by MJF Books
Fine Communications
322 Eighth Avenue
New York, NY 10001

*Ireland's Pirate Queen: The True Story of Grace O'Malley*
LC Control Number 2006938362
ISBN-13: 978-1-56731-858-6
ISBN-10: 1-56731-858-4

Copyright © 1998, 2003 Anne Chambers
Design and Layout © 2003 Merlin Publishing

This edition published by MJF Books. First edition published by Wolfhound
Press, An Imprint of Merlin Publishing, Ireland, under the title *Granuaile:
Ireland's Pirate Queen, Grace O'Malley c. 1530–1603*.
All rights reserved.

Photographs courtesy of the individuals, institutions,
and agencies noted beneath each picture.

MJF Books and the MJF colophon are trademarks of Fine Creative Media, Inc.

Printed in the United States of America.

QM  10  9  8  7  6  5  4  3  2  1

# Contents

In memory of my grandfather
JAMES CRUISE

# *Acknowledgements*

National Library of Ireland,
Public Record Office of Ireland
Genealogical Office of Ireland
Celtic Studies Department, UCD,
Royal Irish Academy,
Trinity College Library,
National Monuments Section, Office of Public Works,
Dublin.
The Public Record Office, London.
Lambeth Palace Library, London.
Hatfield House, Herts.
Lord Sligo, Westport House.
Mr. Gaisford St Lawrence, Howth Castle.
Ms Mairin Ni Dhomhnalláin, Royal Irish Academy.
Mr Kenneth Nicholls, UCC
Mr Jonathan Williams

# *Author's Note*

It is over twenty years since the first edition of *Ireland's Pirate Queen* was published. Since its publication in 1979, the book has been in constant print, and the popularity of the subject has been reflected in its success.

It seems that every year since, I have become involved in other exciting and varied projects about Granuaile: Documentaries for TV and radio, the most recent a drama-documentary for the Discovery Channel in 2003; innumerable articles for books and magazines, interviews and lectures, dance dramas, musicals and ballads; Shaun Davey's evocative *Granuaile Suite*; a Granuaile website; helping a sculptor to encapture Granuaile's likeness in a life-size bronze statue; an interpretative centre based on her life and times; the launching of a new ferry bearing her name; a feature film screenplay. The number and range of undertakings associated with her seem never-ending. Granuaile, it seems, has captured the imagination of everyone who reads about her, just as she captured mine.

Over the years I have come to realise how much I owe her. It is fair to say that she has changed my life, leading me on my own voyage of self-discovery, making me abandon one career midstream for the precarious life of a writer, sending me halfway around the world to tell her story from Connemara to Kingston, introducing me to people in every walk of life, many, through her, have become friends.

It is in an effort to repay this undoubted debt that made me embark on this new edition of her biography. There are, however, more practical reasons which prompted me also. *Ireland's Pirate Queen* was my first book. Now after twenty years and some half-dozen books under my 'quill', I feel that I may have honed away sufficiently at whatever writing skill I possess to attempt to do justice to her story. With the passing years I have got to know and perhaps understand Granuaile more than I did then and am less in awe and more in empathy with her now.

Since 1979, I have had access to some additional information relating to her, particularly among the original manuscript collection in Westport House and also in the archives of public institutions such as the Public Record Office, the Royal Irish Academy and the Department of Celtic Studies, UCD. I found additional information also among the English State Papers of the period, not least another petition of hers written in 1595.

Combined with these new revelations, I wanted to re-examine and analyse her life and the contribution she made to her time in a more comprehensive way, especially in the context of womens's role in history, both political and social. Also the relationship between women and the sea (so much part of both the fact and the legend of Granuaile) and which still appears a barrier, as little breached by modern-day woman as it was in the time of Granuaile, was an added incentive.

And what emerges with greater clarity and assurance than

ever is the life of a unique mould-breaker – a woman far more liberated and empowered than any in this age of perceived equality, with its female heads of state and astronauts, corporate businesswomen and female legislators. Perhaps most intriguing of all is the fact that Granuaile succeeded in competing within the male-oriented environment in which she operated without appearing to jettison her femininity. Her success and notoriety were not achieved at the expense of her womanhood. On the contrary she maximised and utilised her feminine attributes and enjoyed the pleasures her womanhood conferred through her marriages, motherhood and sexual fulfilment – surely the exemplification of a true feminist.

I hope that this biography does justice to this remarkable woman.

Anne Chambers
Dublin 2003

# Introduction

> There came to me also a most feminine sea captain called
> Granny Imallye and offered her services unto me,
> wheresoever I would command her, with three galleys and
> two hundred fighting men, either in Scotland or Ireland.
> She brought with her her husband for she was as well by sea
> as by land well more than Mrs Mate with him.... This was
> a notorious woman in all the coasts of Ireland.
>
> *Sir Henry Sidney, Lord Deputy of Ireland, 1576*

This tantalising description is one of many descriptions in
the Elizabethan State Papers of a most remarkable Irish
woman. To the sixteenth century English administrators
and military men who firstly by persuasion and later by the
sword came to conquer the land of her birth, this 'notorious
woman' provoked awe, anger, revulsion and admiration.
But in Ireland for over four hundred years she was destined
to remain a prisoner of indifference as Irish history chose to
ignore her unique contribution to the social, political and
maritime history of her time. But folklore, poetry and
fiction showed no such bias and must be congratulated for
preserving the memory of one of the most remarkable
women of history, Gráinne (Grace) O'Malley, or as she is
more familiarly known in Ireland, Granuaile.

Like her sisters Granuaile was a victim of the mainly

male orientation of historical record and analyses. But in her case more than mere male chauvinism ensured her dismissal from the pages of history. By not fitting the mould determined and demanded by later generations of Irish historians, Granuaile committed an additional transgression. Until relatively recently, Irish heroes and heroines were required to be suitably adorned in the green cloak of patriotism, their personal lives untainted, their religious beliefs fervently Roman Catholic, with an occasional allowance made for rebel Protestants. Granuaile, as one of her male detractors wrote of her, 'a woman who overstepped the part of womanhood'[2], who allowed neither, religious, social nor political convention to deter her during her lifetime, did not readily fit the required mould.

There are many aspects of her life that could qualify her as *persona non grata* in the roll-call of Irish heroes. She brazingly superseded her husband in his anointed role as chieftain, thereby contravening Salic law on which Gaelic succession was based. She assumed personal command of her father's fleet of galleys and was accepted as undisputed leader, living in close proximity with her hardbitten, all-male crews. She traded and pirated successfully for the space of fifty years from Ireland to Scotland, probably as far afield as Spain. She led rebellions against individual English administrators when they tried to curb her activities, yet allied with the Queen of England when it was to her political advantage. She attacked her own son when he dared to side with her enemy, trained another son so well in the art of survival that he fought with the English forces at the Battle of Kinsale, the last stand of the Gaelic world that bred and bore her. Granuaile allowed neither social nor political convention to deter her ambition. She took a lover, divorced a husband, gave birth to her youngest son on board her ship at sea, made no distinction as to nationality when plundering Irish, English or Spanish ships. Granuaile, the 'chief commander and director of thieves and murderers at sea'[3], hardly fitted the rosy-hued picture of Gaelic womanhood painted by latter-day male and often clerical historians.

Her role in the history of the sixteenth century was allowed lapse into the realm of folklore and fiction. It is notable that the *Annals of the Four Masters*, that seminal source of Irish history, compiled shortly after her death and in a place where memories of her activities were still verdant, does not even mention her name. The English State Papers, on the other hand, contain references to her as late as 1627, some twenty-four years after her death. Such bias erased from the pages of Irish history one of the most remarkable women of the past and by so doing diminished our understanding of the period.

However, it is a measure of Granuaile's greatness that her memory at least was preserved by legend and by folklore. Legends are not created about insignificant people. To be remembered in folk memory is as much a tribute to the impact she made in her life than any academic treatise. As to the factual evidence, it was left to the English administrators and generals, who came to conquer Ireland during her lifetime, to record aspects of the extraordinary role she played. These Elizabethan documents, are now faded and brittle, their age-darkened, spider-like handwriting evidence of the passage of four hundred years since their authors put quill to parchment. From the swirls and flourishes of these sixteenth-century scribes the story of Gráinne O'Malley springs to life. When the factual evidence relating to her life is examined within the context of the traumatic times in which she lived, she emerges as a fearless leader, by land and by sea, a political pragmatist and tactician, a ruthless plunderer, a mercenary, a rebel, a shrewd and able negotiator, the protective matriarch of her family and tribe, the genuine inheritor of the Mother Goddess and Warrior Queen traits of her remote ancestors and, above all else, a woman who broke the mould and played a unique role in history.

The story of Granuaile is the story of one remarkable woman's quest for survival and fulfilment, by land and by sea, in a time of profound political upheaval and male chauvinistic bias. When launching this new edition of her biography, the Tanaiste, Mary Harney TD, described Granuaile as "...the original trail-blazer and mould-breaker. It is only now," she added, "that women were beginning to achieve in politics, business and in the maritime field, the goal set for them four hundred years ago by Grace O'Malley."

# CHAPTER ONE

# Powerful by Land and Sea

*Duine maith riamh ní raibh*
*D'iabh Máille acht 'n a mharaidhe;*
*Fáidhe ne síne sibh-sí,*
*Dine baidhe is bhraithirrí.*

A good man never was there
Of the O'Malleys but a mariner,
The prophets of the weather are ye,
A hospitable and brotherly clan.

O'Dugan (d.1372)

Granuaile was born into the clan Uí Mháille, a hardy, seafaring people on the west coast of Ireland. According to the ancient genealogies of Ireland, the O'Malleys were descended from the eldest son of a High King of Ireland, Brian Orbsen, who was killed at the battle of Dam Chluain, near Tuam, County Galway, circa A.D.388. They were hereditary lords of the region called the Umhalls (umhall meaning territory), later anglicised as the Owles, a territory which comprised the baronies of Murrisk on the south shore of Clew Bay and Burrishoole on the north. The barony of Murrisk, called Umhall Uachtarach or Upper Owel, included the islands of Clare, Inishturk, Caher, Inishbofin, Inishark and a multitude of smaller islands within Clew Bay. The barony of Burrishoole was called Umhall Iochtarach or Lower Owel and originally included the island of Achill. The two baronies were generally referred to as 'Umhall Uí Mháille' (territory of the O'Malleys) or the Owles of O'Malley.

1

In 1235, however, the Anglo-Norman De Burgos invaded Connaught and in a great demonstration of military power swept aside the fragmented Gaelic opposition. In the transition of land and power that followed, the Botiller or Butlers were granted some of the O'Malley territory of Umhall Iochtaracht, the barony of Burrishoole, known as Leath Fherghuis, Fergus's half – Fergus being head of one of the three O'Malley septs. They built a castle there known as Tyrenmore, near Burrishoole Abbey. The Butlers in turn were later dispossessed of the barony of Burrishoole by the sept of Ulick de Burgo, with the exception of Achill, which reverted back to the O'Malleys.

The O'Malleys lived in relative harmony with their de Burgo neighbours becoming their allies in war. In 1342, the de Burgos, like many of their fellow Normans, renounced their allegiance to the English crown and adopted Gaelic names and customs. They divided into two branches, the Mayo Bourkes who adopted the title MacWilliam Iochtarach (i.e the Lower Mac William) and the Galway Burkes who became known as the MacWilliam Uachtarach (the upper MacWilliam). The O'Malley chieftain gave his daughter Sabina in marriage to the new MacWilliam of Mayo. Unlike the other sub-chieftains under the MacWilliam, the O'Malley chieftain paid no rent in tribute to his powerful overlord but merely a 'rising out of six score bands to be maintained by himself, but they have maintenance for the first night from MacWilliam'. [1]

The earliest written reference to the O'Malley territory of Umhall is in the fifth century with the ascent by St Patrick of the spectacular conical mountain then known as Cruachan Aigle (Eagle Mountain). In Tireacháin's note on the life of the saint, contained in the *Book of Armagh*, was written:

'And Patrick went to Mount Egli to fast on it for forty days and forty nights, keeping the discipline of Moses, Elias and Christ. And his charioteer died in Muirisc Aigli, that is the plain between the sea and Aicill and he buried the charioteer, Totmael and piled stones as a sepulchre...'[2]

Patrick's pilgrimage in 441 A.D. is commemorated annually by thousands of people who walk in his footsteps to the summit of the mountain that now bears his name.

The rugged, scenic splendour of the Umhalls moved William Makepeace Thackeray to write in 1842. 'It forms an event in one's life to have seen that place, so beautiful is it and so unlike all other beauties that I know of'.[3] The territory is encompassed by the towering peak of Croagh Patrick to the south, Mweelrea, Croaghmore on Clare Island and Slievemore on Achill to the west and the Nephin range to the north. At its heart is the broad expanse of the island-strewn Clew Bay, that 'miracle of beauty', with Clare Island, a Sphinx-like bulwark against the surge of the wild Atlantic ocean that stretches away towards the western horizon. The Umhalls comprised some fertile land around Belclare and Murrisk and wide tracts of bog, marsh, rough mountain grazing and extensive woodland. Apart from its scenic beauty, this sea-washed territory of the Umhalls was an appropriate base for a seafaring clan.

Although an island, Ireland has produced few seafaring families of note. The O'Malleys differed from the majority of Irish clans in that they dervived their living mainly from the sea. Their clan motto, *'terra marique potens'* (powerful by land and sea) proclaimed them lords of the seas around Ireland. In the ancient *Book of Rights (Leabhar ne gCeart)* which lists the rights and tributes paid to the King of Connaught, it is recorded that 'the command of the fleet to O'Flaherti and O'Mali, whenever he (the king) goes on sea or on the high sea'.[4] O'Malley paid the King at his residence at Cruachan a yearly tribute of 'one hundred milch cows, one hundred hogs and one hundred casks of beer.' The King, in return for O'Malley's service, tributes and loyalty, presented him with the substantial annual gift of 'five ships, five horses, five swords and five corselets'.[5]

Like many coastal families, the O'Malleys claimed a traditional lordship of their immediate sea territory which included the right to levy tolls for safe passage and the right to sell fishing rights to foreign fleets. Writing in 1579, one English administrator sought to abolish this custom.

> 'Towards the sea coast there lieth many fair islands, rich and plentiful of all commodities, there cometh hither every year likely about fifty English ships for fishing. They have been compelled to pay a great tribute to the O'Malleys...'[6]

But unlike most coastal families, the O'Malleys were themselves intrepid seafarers, whose seafaring was not confined to Ireland. A verse of a fifteenth-century poem confirms what tradition also maintained - that they traded and plundered as far as Spain and Scotland.

> *Leomhain an oirir uaine*
> *eolaigh oirir na Spáinne*
> *ag buain chruidh do Ceann Tíre*
> *gearr míle ar muir d'ibh Máille*

> They are the lions of the green sea
> men acquainted with the land of Spain
> when seizing cattle from Kintyre
> a mile by sea is short to the O'Malleys.[7]

In 1123, the earliest mention of the name Uí Máille appears in the *Annals of the Four Masters* which records that 'Tadhg Ua Maille lord of Umhall was drowned with his ship at Aran.'[8] From then the name appears frequently in historical records, usually in connection with the clan's seafaring exploits. In 1413 the annals record how Tuathal O'Malley returned home from mercenary service in Ulster

> 'with seven ships and their crews....a storm arose on the western sea, which drove them to the right towards Scotland, where six of the ships, with all their crews were sunk... Tuathal, himself with much difficulty effected a landing in Scotland.'[9]

The annals state that 244 of Tuathal's crewmen were drowned in the tragedy, an indication of his substantial following and seapower. It was this Tuathal O'Malley who, on being wounded in a quarrel with a poet, instead of claiming an *eric* (the legal payment for bloodshed) chose instead to have the poet compose a poem for him. It is an insight not only into the cultural obverse of the warlike Gaelic chief, but also an acknowledgement as to how prized poetry was in the Gaelic world. In his bardic verses, the poet eulogised Tuathal and praised him for his choice.

> You did not claim a pledge for your wound
> You ignored the loss of the best blood
> Here to requite you for it is a melodious poem
> You deserved from me the price of your healing. [10]

It required a special measure of skill and daring to extract a living from the sea along the formidable Atlantic seaboard. The sea routes north to Scotland and south to the Continent, along the indented western coastline, were

hazardous. They were made even more so by impediments
such as basic navigational aids, the absence of well-defined
charts, wooden-hulled ships and the ever present threat of
piracy. But their mobility by sea gave the O'Malleys distinct
advantages over their land-bound neighbours. It provided
them with an escape route from their enemies in time of
attack, an advantage availed of later by Granuaile and her
sons. It allowed them access to foreign markets to sell their
produce in exchange for goods unavailable at home. It is
reasonable to assume that over the centuries O'Malley
castles were bedecked with more exotic furnishings than
their neighbours and their table replenished with the wines
of France and Spain. Less tangible but nonetheless
advantageous was an opportunity denied most of their land-
bound contemporaries, to mingle with other peoples and
cultures, to observe, to learn, to glean knowledge of events
in the wider world outside Ireland. To seafaring folk, like the
O'Malleys, the sea was always a highway while landlubbers
saw it only as a barrier.

Recent research on trade links between Ireland and the
Continent has confirmed what tradition has always held,
that from the Middle Ages, Irish owned ships, manned by
Irish crews regularly crossed the seas to ports in England,
France and Spain. The ports along the west coast of Ireland
tended to trade with Bristol in England, ports on the west
coast of France and on the coast of Galicia in northern
Spain. For a sea-going clan like the O'Malleys, there was
another incentive for them to trade their produce in foreign
markets. Galway city was the centre of trade on the west
coast and by the early sixteenth century was described as
'one of the first emporia of trade, not only in Ireland, but
with few exceptions, in the British isles as well'.[11] But the
wealthy merchant families who ruled the city had enacted a

series of restrictive by-laws which prohibited non-residents, particularly the Gaelic clans, outside the city walls, from trading there. Trade in wool, the mainstay of most Gaelic clans, was also prohibited. In 1460, the Corporation of the city had enacted

> ...that ne merchent, ne maryner, ne shipman, should unlode, ne transport over the seas, unfremans goods, but only fremans, upon paine to lesse the said goods or the just value therof and to forfoyte 100 shillings.[12]

Coupled with the racist sentiment of an 1518 by-law, which fined citizens who entertained their Gaelic neighbours within the city without licence of the mayor and council on any feast day, so 'that neither O' ne Mac shall strutte ne swagger thru the streets of Galway',[13] made it imperative for the O'Malleys to sail with their produce, free from taxes and restrictions to foreign markets from their own ports, like Cathair-na-mart and Clare Island.

Fishing was one of the clan's main sources of income. The fishing grounds off the coast of O'Malley's lordship were considered one of the most fertile in Ireland. Herring was the principal species caught, with hake, cod, ling, turbot, salmon and shellfish. The fish was usually salted, sometimes dried and packed in wooden barrels for export. Hides, tallow, freize cloth, deer and sheepskins, furs such as pinemarten, considered a highly fashionable accessory in the sixteenth century, coney, fox and otter were other important commodities from the west of Ireland which found a ready market abroad.

Fishing, however, was not the sole maritime activity of the clan. As in most coastal communities, plundering and piracy had supplemented the O'Malley income from earliest times. The ancient annals record with regular

monotony O'Malley raids on outlying coastal settlements
from Kerry to Donegal.

> 'Eogan O'Máille went with the crews of three ships
> against Cille bega (Killybegs, Co. Donegal) in the
> night...They raid and burn the town and take many
> prisoners'.[14]

Granuaile who indulged in the profession with more success
than perhaps any of her ancestors, was accused of being 'a
chief director and commander of thieves and murderers at
sea',[15] and raided from Scotland to the south coast of
Ireland.

Piracy has been in existence for over five thousand years,
from ancient Persia to modern-day China. Every known
civilisation through the ages has produced a pirate
community. Depending on mainly political and, to a lesser
degree, cultural considerations, piracy has been viewed
pragmatically by rulers down through the centuries. 'The
Ancient Greeks and Carthaginians had no qualms about
piracy being proper conduct'.[16] The Vikings used it as a
means of establishing footholds in Ireland, Britain and the
Continent. In the Red Sea, the Persian Gulf and all along
the north African coast, piracy flourished throughout
history. In the Far East it was undertaken in a massive scale
and still exists today. Granuaile's great contemporary,
Queen Elizabeth I, gave her letters of marque to the pirate
turned privateer, Sir Francis Drake, when it seemed likely
that his unlawful activities on the high seas would
substantially supplement her state coffers. Despite their
notoriety, it is worth noting that Granuaile's career predated
by a hundred and fifty years the careers of the more widely
known Caribbean women pirates, the Irish-born Ann Bonny
and her companion, Mary Read.

The struggle for power and profit at sea no more than mirrored a similiar struggle on land, but perhaps with more romance and notoriety. Piracy is often a symptom of political chaos on land and in Ireland in the sixteenth century, as the old Gaelic world faced the ultimate assault by a more powerful neighbour and slowly disintegrated, this was very obviously the case. This period saw Granuaile's career at sea reach its zenith. Her strongholds, situated deep within the inlets of Clew bay, inaccessible only to those with a local knowledge of its dangerous channels, tides, currents, reefs and sandbanks, made capture or reprisal for her piracy activities, as it had for her ancestors, virtually impossible. It was not until the end of the sixteenth century when cartographers began to more accurately map the remoter havens of the west coast that time and the English navy caught up with her activities at sea.

There was another string to the O'Malleys' maritime bow. The employment of mercenaries was a common feature of Gaelic warfare. The most renowned were the *galloglaigh* (foreign warriors), anglicised gallowglass, who came from the isles and highlands of Scotland. They were hired annually, usually from May to October, by individual Gaelic chieftains or gaelicised Anglo-Norman lords, to fight their battles against an enemy chieftain or lord. The Clan Donnell was the gallowglass family most associated with the west of Ireland and it was O'Malley ships which ferried them to and from their Scottish homeland. A branch of the Clan Donnell eventually settled permanently in Umhall, as sub-chieftains of the O'Malleys. If the gallowglass were the mercenaries of land, the O'Malleys could well be termed the mercenaries of the sea. O'Malley ships and crews were much sought after for hire by the warring chieftains and, to judge by the many references in the annals to O'Malley involvement in battles and skirmishes in Munster and Ulster, there was no scarcity of work. This mercenary tradition was continued by Granuaile and her sons until the early years of the seventeenth century.

The number and size of the O'Malley fleet has never been precisely quantified. Irish-built trading vessels of the sixteenth century would have been a version of the clinker-built, wooden cog of late medieval times. There are many references to the number of ships under the direction of individual members of the O'Malley clan. Tuathal O'Malley had seven ships under his command in Ulster in 1413, while in 1513 Eoghan O'Malley attacked Killybegs with three ships. Granuaile is recorded as commanding from three to twenty ships during the length of her career.

The 'galley' was the ship most associated with the O'Malleys and particularly with Granuaile. Wooden-hulled and clinker-built, the galley had a shallow draught which allowed it to manoeuvre in low water. Powered by as many as thirty oars and a single sail, it was a speedy and versatile craft. The galley is thought to have evolved from the long ships, 'langskips' of the Vikings, the intrepid seafarers from Scandinavia. The typical Viking ship had a keel, a mast of pine or ash measuring up to 11 metres, a square sail, a single row of oars on either side, a side rudder afixed to the starboard quarter and could attain a speed of up to ten knots. Major developments in boatbuilding practices occurred particularly in the fifteenth century. The single masted ship, difficult to steer and able only to sail with the wind, gave way to lateen rigged two and three masted ships such as the carrack, the galleon, galleas and the galley. The Mediterranean type galley had evolved from the ancient trireme but its once three tiered oar power, by the sixteenth century, had given way to a row of single oars on each side manned by more than one rower. Long and narrow these galleys often had as many as three masts, small decks fore and aft and could accommodate as many as three hundred. Four of these galleys formed part of the Spanish Armada invasion of England of 1588 but were ill-suited to the northern seas.

Experts appear reluctant to accept that the O'Malley galleys were more substantial craft than, for example, the smaller Hebridean galleys, commonly depicted on stone slabs and tombstone carvings. Descriptions of the galleys commanded by Granuaile in the sixteenth century show that they differ substantially in size from those of the Hebrides. Granuaile could offer Sidney in 1576 'three galleys and two hundred fighting men,' capable of sailing anywhere in Ireland or in Scotland. The State Papers further record in 1599

> There are three very good galleys with Tibbott ne Long, son to Grany O'Malley...that will carry 300 men apiece. ...There are no galleys in Ireland but these'.[17]

In 1601 an English sea captain on patrol off the Mayo coast describes a skirmish with one of Granuaile's galleys which was 'rowed with thirty oars and had on board ready to defend her 100 good shot'.[18] All the extant descriptions of Granuaile's galleys point to vessels of considerable size, perhaps a cross between the Hebridean galleys of the north and the galleys of the Mediterranean. What we do know for certain is that they were of such strength, versatility and capability that for the space of fifty years they carried Granuaile and her army of 'two hundred fighting men', plus the plunder she accumulated en route, safely in the most dangerous and unpredictable seas off the coasts of Ireland and Scotland.

In 1991, there was a reinactment of the 400 mile voyage between Clew Bay to the Scottish isle of Stornoway, undertaken many times by both Granuaile and Somerled, Lord of the Isles. The replica galley had sixteen oars, less than half the number recorded on the galleys operated by Granuaile. From descriptions in the State Papers, it would appear that the galleys under Granuaile's command were not only substantial but unique in Ireland. As Colin Mudie, designer of the Brendan and Argo vessels for Tim Severin's epic voyages, as well as Granuaile's replica galley mentioned above, warns,

> 'we... have to look at historic craft not from any vantage point of technological superiority but from a much more humble station, appreciating how little we may know and how much may be to learn'.[19]

For a seafaring clan, part of whose income was dervived from plunder and piracy, it was essential that O'Malley land bases were strategically situated – secure from retaliation as much as sheltered from the elements. The ring of O'Malley castles strung around the shoreline of Clew Bay fulfils these requirements admirable. The seat of the O'Malley chieftain was at Belclare castle (Dún Béal and Chláir – the Fort at the Mouth of the Plain, the plain of Murrisk). It was situated at the mouth of the Owenwee river on the site of an ancient *dún* or fort. Southeast inland from Belclare was a lake dwelling (*crannóg*) on the island in Moher lake, a place of refuge for the chieftain, his family and their valuables in time of danger. The family also possessed a castle at Cathair-na-Mart (Fort of the Beeves), situated alongside the present Westport House, a castle at Murrisk, Carrowmore, west of the present town of Louisburgh, Kildawnet on Achill Island and the castle on Clare Island.

Clare Island and Achill are the only O'Malley castles extant. Although not the main residences of the O'Malley chieftain they afford some insight into the living conditions of a Gaelic clan from about the twelfth century onwards. Both castles are strategically situated with commanding views of the sea, yet are undetectable by passing sea traffic. The castle on Clare Island is situated on a low rocky headland looking eastwards into the broad expanse of Clew Bay. It overlooks a fine crescent sandy beach, very suitable for beaching or mooring ships of shallow draught. Directly below it is a sheltered creek which has deep water at high tide. The castle is three stories high and once possessed battlements which gave an uninterrupted view of the open sea beyond the island. The three floor levels were connected by a stone stairway, straight rather than spiral, the more usual defensive access in these type of structures. The strong rectangular castle of Kildawnet is situated on a slight promontory on the west shore of Achill Sound. The Sound, with its strong and unpredictable currents, is a sea-passage which connects Clew Bay with Blacksod Bay to the north. With local knowledge it provided short and swift access, or escape, north or south between Achill Island and the mainland. The entrance to the Sound at the south end is protected by the island of Achill Beg. The castle itself is quite hidden from view from the outer sea and is surrounded by mountain and seascapes of the wildest splendour.

Like other Gaelic clans before the Reformation, the O'Malleys sustained orders of monks on their lands. The abbey at Murrisk was built by the O'Malleys in 1457 for the Augustinian friars, on land granted by the chieftain Thady O'Malley. It is beautifully situated on a quiet inlet of Clew Bay, beneath the towering peak of Croagh Patrick. Built in late Gothic style, its single aisle church and a range of domestic buildings are now in semi-ruin. One of its best preserved features is the delicate east window with its interlacing bar tracery and five trefoil parts. A striking feature of the abbey is its turreted south wall. At the west end of the church a partly vaulted tower once stood. After the initial account of its foundation, ironically nothing more was recorded about the abbey until notice of its proposed supression on 27 March 1574, when Sir Peter Carew, in a despatch to the English Lord Deputy in Ireland, mentioned 'the abbey of Moyriske possessed by Friars or rebels so as her Majestie hath no commoditie in the same'.[20] In 1578, the Queen leased the lands of the abbey to James Garvey. The friars, however, continued in residence for sometime longer. In 1635 a chalice was presented to them inscribed. 'Pray for the souls of Theobald, Lord Viscount Mayo and his wife Maeve Ne Cnochoure who had me made for the monestary of Mureske in the year of our lord 1635.' (Theobald or Tibbott-ne-Long Bourke was the son of Granuaile.) Murrisk Abbey would have featured largely in the lives of the O'Malley chieftains, being situated close to Belclare. It is perhaps likely that Granuaile may have been baptised and married there, and many of her ancestors and descendants lie buried beneath its now roofless walls.

The abbey on Clare Island was built by the O'Malleys two centuries before Murrisk, in 1224. Originally a Carmelite cell, it was later attached to the Cistercian house at Knockmoy. The later fifteenth century church consisted of a nave, chancel and sacristy, as well as a range of domestic buildings to the north of the chapel which no longer exist. On the roof of the chancel are one of the most unusual features of the abbey thought, following recent research and preservation, to date from the fourteenth century. The paintings, which once covered the entire ceiling, in a kaleidoscope of colour, depict mythical, human and animal figures, including dragons, a cockerel, stags, men on foot and on horseback, a harper, birds and trees. On the north wall of the chancel is a well-cut undated limestone slab showing a stallion salient on a wreath above a Norman-style helmet, a wild boar trippant in the centre, with three bows with arrows affixed, pointing at the boar. At the right-hand base is a replica galley, with furled sail and five oars on a side, with the name 'O'Maille' and the motto *'Terra Mariq Potens'* in smaller lettering above. The entire shield and crest is surrounded by mantling and is thought to date from the early seventeenth century. Beside the slab is a tomb canopy, with elegant cusped tracery, which although recent research suggests dates from the fourteenth century, tradition has always held to be the burial place of Granuaile. The Norman-style helmet on the stone slab could possibly have relevance to Granuaile's second husband, Richard Bourke, the Mayo MacWilliam. The memorial and slab seem somewhat incongruous in such a remote and humble setting and, if tradition is to be believed, is indeed a fitting resting place for Granuaile.

After the initial setback at the hands of the De Burgos in the twelfth century, by which the jurisdiction of the O'Malley chieftains became restricted to Umhall Uachtarach and Achill, they continued their seafaring activities with renewed vigour. By the sixteenth century they were, as the English State Papers acknowledge, 'much feared everywhere by sea'.[21] Politically they continued as an independent clan, the O'Malley chieftain being the only Gaelic chieftain in Mayo to retain his rank until the extinction of the title in the seventeenth century.

# Chapter Two

# The World of Granuaile

... men of sense
Hand down that Muireasc surely has its name,
From lovely Muirisc of the snowly hands,
The daughter of great Hugony the King,
She was a downright beauty, daring, bold,
And fixed her habitation near this bay,
Beneath the base of Cruachan Aigli, where
She ruled o'er hardy sailors and great men.[1]

The lines of this ancient poem eulogise a remote woman leader called Muirisc, from whom the O'Malley Barony of Murrisk is said to have taken its name. Nothing more is known about her, but from the historical records it is obvious that in a prophetic way Muirisc's life presaged that of her sixteenth century descendant, Granuaile, acknowledged leader also 'o'er hardy sailors and great men', over one thousand years later.

This connection between two women from the same remote lordship, more than a millennium apart, is not so strange as it may appear. The warrior woman Muirisc lived in a time when Ireland was part of a Bronze-Age matriarchal culture in which the dominant deities were women. The name of Ireland itself is that of the mother-goddess Eriu or Eire, said to be one of the three legendary goddesses who ruled the country at the time of the invasion of the Milesians. The mystical Tuatha de Danaan, worshipped by the pagan Irish, had the all-powerful

16

goddess Dana as their deity. In early Irish mythology the sovereignty of Ireland *Flaitheas Éireann* was epitomised by a woman, invariably dressed in a blue cloak. Later still the Celtic culture of the late Iron Age, which gave rise to the heroic legends of Fionn mac Cumhal and the Fenians and the Red Branch Knights of Ulster, the dominance of the woman warrior class was still very much in evidence. The prime hero of the Red Branch cycle, Cuchulainn, learned his battle prowess under the tutelage of the woman warrior Scathach. In combat he could overcome the warrior Princess Aoife only by resorting to trickery. Classical writers testified to the fighting skills of Celtic women. The Roman historian Tacitus confirmed that the Celts of Britain made no distinction as to sex in the choice of their military commanders, as in the case of Boudica. The warrior queen Maeve of Connaught, was a powerful and fearless woman who was prepared to go to war to achieve her ambition. Many of the warriors of the heroic legends of the Fenian and Ulster cycles used their mother's name in place of a patronymic (as the king of Ulster, Conor Mac (son of) Nessa), reinforcing the idea that in earlier times in Ireland descent was accomplished through the female line.

The demise in Ireland of a society ruled by powerful, warrior women coincided with the advent of Christianity and the influence of Roman law which accompanied it. Roman society was male-dominated, the male having ultimate power over the lives of his dependent household, including women, and also over his slaves on which Roman society was based. Descent was exclusively patrilineal and inheritance strictly confined to the legitimate male heir. Christianity both inherited and defended this system. The writings of the early Christian saints such as Paul, John, Ambrose, Jerome and Augustine, reflected the degraded position of women in Roman society. Augustine wrote of the 'horrible beastliness of women', that they were not born in God's image and should barely be tolerated on sufferance, let alone fill any position of authority. As Roman law and the Christian ethos began to dominate, this negative attitude towards women in society became enshrined in both state and religious laws and customs across Europe. By the sixteenth century male historians and commentators, often clerical, perpetuated this attitude to women. However, amidst their reassertion of women's inferiority, weakness and unsuitability for high office, either in church or state, often lurked a fear which occasionally and inadvertantly revealed man's acknowledgement of women's true potential. In his condemnation of their role in politics, in which he accused women of being 'the cause of many troubles, have done great harm to those that govern cities, and have caused in them many divisions...,'[2], the sixteenth-century political analyst, Niccolo Machiavelli, for example, involuntarily acknowledges their ability.

The Romans overcame Celtic nations from Asia Minor right across to Britain. Only Ireland remained outside Roman influence. Patrick brought Christianity to Ireland in the fifth century, and with it Roman law, which found itself in direct conflict with the indigenous law of Ireland, known as Brehon law. With Ireland's established tradition of a matriarchical culture, on no issue did both laws differ so fundamentally than on the status of women. Gradually as Christianity infiltrated native Irish law, women's role in the power stakes in Ireland was diluted. Roman salic law, which debarred women from leadership, became part of Brehon law. Gradually but insidiously the role of women was confined to childbearing, engaging in charitable deeds, for which they were occasionally lauded in the Irish annals, and being subservient to their husbands. In succeeding centuries in Ireland, while individual women, like Gormflaith, Dervogilla, Margaret Fitzgerald, Countess of Ormond, Eleanor Butler, Countess of Desmond, Fionnula Mac Donnell *Iníon Dubh*, managed to come to political prominence, it tended to be within the orbit of their husbands' or lovers' power struggles. By the time of Granuaile in the sixteenth century, an analogy for an independent woman ruler could be found only in myth and legend. This in turn caused the life of Granuaile herself to be relegated to myth, rather than to acknowledge that a woman could usurp what had by then become to be accepted as the exclusive role of man.

While Granuaile's career as a political leader by land can be said to mirror her Celtic woman ancestors, no such analogy can be found to explain her unique role as leader by sea. The sea and seafaring has from the beginning of time been considered a male preserve and piracy one of the bastions of male domination. From the legendary odysseys of Jason, Ulysses. and Sinbad, to the explorative voyages of Columbus, Da Gama and Magellan to the New Worlds, down to the time of Granuaile's more famous seafaring contemporaries, Frobisher, Drake and Raleigh, a woman's place was not aboard a ship and most definitely not at the helm. Even in this age of 'gender equality', the sea and seafaring has, in the main, tended to continue to be a male preserve. Women commanders in the navies of the modern world are still a rarity. Women on ships were thought to be 'the devil's ballast', a bad omen, fated to bring storms and shipwreck. There was place for only one woman in the sailor's life at sea and that was the sea goddess herself. From pagan Aphrodite to the Christian Mary Star of the Sea, the ocean had to be placated, appeased and venerated to ensure a safe passage for those men who sailed on her heaving bosom. In Ireland, as elsewhere, seafaring was traditionally a male pursuit. Had Granuaile been born her father's son, she would probably not have received notoriety. She would have merely been another O'Malley continuing the long-established seafaring tradition of his clan. The fact that as a woman she simply did just that, makes her both unique and somehow incredulous.

Granuaile was the only child of her parents, Owen 'Dubhdara' (Black Oak) O'Malley, chief of his name and ruler of Umhall Uachtarach, i.e. the Barony of Murrisk. His name conjures up the image of a strong, broad-shouldered, swarthy man, his shoulder-length hair cut in the customary 'glib' or fringe across his forehead. He dressed in tight worsted trews of the period, with a saffron *léine* or shirt, with wide sleeves, under a studded jack of tanned leather. A voluminous woollen cloak, deeply fringed around the neck, fastened with a gold pin, fell in folds around him. On his feet, square-toed brogues and in the leather belt around his waist his *skeyne* or knife. A proud and independent chieftain, Dubhdara O'Malley was one of the few Gaelic chieftains of the time never to have submitted to the English crown.

Granuaile's mother was Margaret, daughter of Conchobhar Og Mac Conchobhair, mic Maoilseachlain O'Malley, of the sept of Moher. According to contemporary English accounts, Gaelic women were

> Very comely creatures, tall, slender and upright. Of complexion very fayre and cleare skinned, but freckled, with tresses of bright yellow hayre, which they chayne up in curious knotts and devises. They are not strait laced nor plated in theyr youth, but suffered to grow at liberty so that you shall hardly see one crooked or deformed, but yet as the proverb is, soone ripe soone

rotten. Theyre propensity to generation causeth that they cannot endure. They are women at thirteen and old wives at thirty....Of nature they are very kind and tractable...[3]

Whether Granuaile or her mother answered to this particular description of Gaelic women is unknown. As wife of a chieftain, Margaret O'Malley dressed in the traditional women's linen *léine*, reaching to the ankles and over this a long tunic with a laced bodice, with perhaps a string of amber beads around her neck. Married women in Gaelic society tended to enfold their heads with a curious rolled linen headcloth. Her duties would have centered on her husband's household, supervising the preparation of food, the upkeep of the castle and the entertainment of her husband's allies and guests.

Granuaile had a brother named Dónal, known as Dónal-na-Piopa (Dónal of the pipes) who was still living at the clan castle of Cathair-na-Mart in 1593. There is evidence to suggest that Dónal was either illegitimate or Granuaile's half-brother by a woman other than her mother. In a bill of chancery, Granuaile's son was later to testify that she was 'the sole heir to the said Margrett',[4] her mother, and that she had inherited Margaret's lands in Umhall. The earliest record of Granuaile's father, Dubhdara O'Malley, occurs in 1549, during the reign of Edward VI in England. In statutes compiled by the king's commissioners in Ireland, which lists the principal chieftains in the country, is the name 'O'Mayle of Pomo'.[5] This is an interesting misnomer. The word *pomo* in Latin means 'apple'. The Irish word *Umhall*, meaning territory, is pronounced similarly to the Irish word for apple, *úll*. Thus O'Malley of Umhall became O'Malley of Pomo in the English state papers.

The landscape of Ireland at the time of Granuaile's birth was virtually unchanged since the Anglo-Norman invasion of the twelfth century. The population is thought to have numbered no more than 7000,000 people. Great primeval forests of oak, birch, ash, scots fir, hazel, willow, alder and holly and dense woodlands covered a sizeable part of the countryside. There were large tracts of marsh and boglands interspaced by arable and open pasture lands. There were few roads and even fewer bridges. Most of the towns were situated on the coast or on the navigable rivers. Because of the absence of roads and bridges, travel was extremely difficult and there was much recourse to travel by water, both by river and sea. The mountain pass, the forest pathway and the river ford were the all-important keys to communication and their control were often the source of warfare. Behind a natural screen of forest, water and mountain the Gaelic world flourished. There were no accurate maps of the country and successive English kings who had claimed lordship over Ireland since the twelfth century, knew as little about the country as they did about the far-off Americas. The actual mapping of Ireland towards the end of the sixteenth century was a major contributory factor to the eventual submission of the Gaelic world at the beginning of the seventeenth century. The maps were in themselves symbols of the extension of English control.

Granuaile was born at the beginning of an era which was to prove a milestone in the history of Ireland. The effects of the Anglo-Norman invasion of the twelfth century were by then scarcely evident. English power was confined to Dublin and the Pale, a small area stretching north, south and west of the city. The native Irish held all Ulster, with the exception of parts of Down and Antrim, most of Connaught, the north and west of Munster, the midlands and west Leinster. The native customs, laws and language, which had received a reversal at the time of the invasion, flourished again. Even the descendants of the Anglo Norman dynasties like the earls of Kildare, Desmond, Ormond and the De Burgos in Connaught, had become gaelicised, becoming 'more Irish than the Irish themselves' to varying degrees, depending on their political and geographical proximity to Dublin.

At the time of Granuaile's birth, Ireland was divided into as many as

> ...sixty counties...where reigneth sixty chief captains...that liveth only by the sword and obeyeth to no other temporal person but only to himself that is strong. And every of the said captains maketh war and peace for himself and holdeth by the sword and hath imperial jurisdiction within his room and obeyeth to no other person, English or Irish, except only to such persons as may subdue him by the sword.[6]

In England, a few decades earlier, the Tudors had succeeded in bringing the powerful feudal magnates to heel, claiming a divine right to rule over them as kings. In Ireland, no similar central authority had emerged to mould the regained power of the individual chieftains and gaelicised Anglo–Norman lords into a viable and strong centralised government. Instead inter-clan warfare, which was to be the achilles heel of Gaelic resistence to England later in the century, prevailed.

Granuaile's father, as one of the 'sixty captains' referred to, ruled the lordship of Umhall, according to native Brehon law. The Gaelic legal system was distinct to Ireland and had evolved over the centuries from its Celtic origins, absorbing some aspects of the two main outside incursions –

Christianity in the fifth century and the Anglo–Norman invasion with its feudal laws in the twelfth century. The very nature of Gaelic society and its capacity to assimulate foreign influences, had made it resilient. Gaelic society comprised clans or extended family groupings of independent chieftaincies. The chieftain was elected by members of the ruling sept or family within the clan and did not inherit by feudal primogeniture. By Gaelic law a brother could succeed a brother, a nephew an uncle, a younger son a father to the chieftaincy. A custom known as 'tanistry' had been introduced whereby the elected successor *taniste* to the chieftain was chosen during the chieftain's lifetime. The Salic law, which prohibited women from being eligible for election, was, by the sixteenth century, well–established. The tenure of land also differed from the feudal system and was conducted according to a complex method of land distribution, differing from region to region, whereby on the death of a chieftain, or a co–heir or, in some areas on an annual basis each May Day, the clan lands were redistributed among the ruling or landholding members of the clan. The chieftain enjoyed a life interest only in the lands pertaining to the chieftaincy. The fosterage of the sons of an overlord with a sub–lord was a common practice and further strengthened the links of dependency between them. Sons born outside wedlock were not discriminated against either socially or legally. They were eligible for election to the chieftaincy and enjoyed the same inheritance rights as sons born within wedlock.

The chieftain's power was based on a system of clientship, *célsine*, whereby he strove to have as many *úir–rí* (sub–lords) under his control. In lieu of his protection, his sub–lords were required to pay him onerous dues and tributes, such as a specific annual payment of cattle, sheep, grain, flour, honey or candles, the provision of lodging and entertainment, known as cuddy *cuid oíche*, for the chieftain and his retinue. They were also obliged to fulfil specific duties, including the provision of a 'rising out' (an agreed number of armed men) to assist the overlord in war, as the O'Malley chieftain provided to his overlord, the MacWilliam Bourke. Likewise the O'Malley chieftain was in receipt from his sublords in Umhall, the MacGibbons and the Clandonnells, 'the chief rents of barley, butter and money as well as all fines for bloodshed, all skins of animals killed or to be killed... with all customs and other casualties'[7].

Debarred from the chieftaincy and therefore from power, Gaelic woman, as the annals confirm, were rarely acknowledged other than as wives of chieftains, doers of charitable works, donaters of bequests to abbeys and monasteries and occasionally as patrons of educational establishments. Politically some featured in the background as disruptive or negative influences in the politics being pursued by their husbands or lovers, such as the infamous Dervogilla O'Rourke. Some like Eleanor Butler FitzGerald, Countess of Desmond, and Margaret FitzGerald Butler, Countess of Ormond, filled the vacuum caused by their husband's political inadequacies but received little official acknowledgement in the process. While Gaelic law mitigated against women in the political sense, in other respects, particularly in the area of marriage and divorce, it accorded them much more protection and many more rights than their European counterparts. They could retain their maiden names during their marriage(s). Granuaile herself testified to the fact (see appendex V1) that the dowry, or marriage portion, women brought on marriage to their husbands, was protected by law and was refundable on death or divorce. However she did complain that such dowries were refundable to women only on a first marriage. (As she married twice, she got around this impediment by simply taking over her second husband's castle in lieu!) Irish law also permitted women, like Granuaile and her mother before her, to own and administer their own land and property, a practice which contrasted sharply with English law where a husband enjoyed absolute control over his wife's property. In a late sixteenth-century poem composed in honour of Granuaile's son, Tibott-ne-Long (Tibóid na Long) Bourke, it is notable that he is referred to as 'the ruddy-cheeked heir of Gráinne'[8] his mother, rather than his father, as would be more usually expected, a further indication that Granuaile was a proprietor in her own right.

As well as the ruling class, Gaelic society was comprised of freemen and landless labourers, referred to alternatively as betagh *biatach* or churls. The betagh were the backbone of Gaelic society. They worked from dawn to dusk for their chieftain and received few privileges in return. There was also the learned class *aes dána* which included the poets *filí*, the most revered of all classes, the bards and the dispensers of law, the brehons *breitheamh* or judges. There were two classes of military men, the gallowglass and the kern *ceithearn*. The gallowglass were, as previously mentioned, mercenary soldiers from the Scottish isles and highlands. Of great strength and stature, the gallowglass dressed from neck to heel in chain mail, conical, iron helmets and were armed with great swords and the infamous battleaxe. The kerne were the light infantry of the chieftain's army. Armed with bows and arrows, javelins and darts, their speed and agility were of special importance on marshy land where they could outrun and outmanoeuvre even enemy horsemen. Gaelic forces seldom fought in military formation. They attacked by making rapid and irregular forays then withdrawing, using their knowledge of the terrain, the woodland, forest, marsh and bog, tactically to their advantage. Prior to the Elizabethan conquest of the country, interclan rivalry, disputes over succession to the chieftaincy and cattle raiding were the principal causes of inter-clan warfare.

Despite the Reformation in England, Ireland still adhered to the old religion. Gaelic Catholicism, however, differed greatly from that of the Roman church. The sweeping reforms of previous centuries had, by and large, failed to make much impression on its structure and ethos and the Gaelic church adhered to many practices of its Celtic pagan roots. A chieftain's coronation ceremony was not conducted in a church but at the pagan rath of his remote ancestors. A pattern of hereditary clergy had evolved where members of a particular family, often non-clerical, were invested with abbacies and bishoprics. Some of the clergy, including bishops and abbots, were either married or maintained concubines. Many of the aristocratic families sought and were given licence to marry within the prohibited degrees of consanguinity. A form of Celtic secular marriage prevailed. Trial marriages were commonplace and divorce was long established as a legal right. The sacraments were celebrated haphazardly and many of the clergy were illiterate.

The living conditions of Gaelic chieftains were geared to the predominantly agrarian and military lifestyle they pursued, a feature reflected in the construction of their dwellings, which were built primarily for shelter and defence rather than for comfort. Before the advent of cannon, such structures were virtually impossible to capture. Dubhdara O'Malley lived in the stone fortress of Belclare, a somewhat larger edition of the castles of Clare Island and Kildawnet. These castles or towers were four or

five stories high with a bawn, enclosed by high walls, often
with a small barbican protecting the entrance. The castle
was lit by narrow slit windows, called loops, and had turrets
and crenellations below the roof, usually made of thatch,
occassionally of lead. The castle was dark and damp inside,
especially the lower floors, which were used mainly for
storage. The chieftain and his family lived in the upper
apartments which were brighter and often had a fireplace.
The walls were whitewashed and hung with antlers, skins
and green-leaved branches. The furniture was minimal and
basic; wooden tables, benches, presses and bedsteads.
Around the outskirts of the castle nestled the beehive
dwellings of the chieftain's followers. While remains of the
stone fortresses of the chieftains dot the Irish landscape, few
if any examples of the dwellings of the landless majority
have survived. Writing at the turn of this century, a visitor
to Achill island saw one of the last surviving examples of
these ancient dwellings and wrote that they comprised a

> low circular room, thatched outside but within ceiled
> with stout rafters, a massive bog pine pillar in the
> centre holds up the roof. There is a low door, no
> window and a small hole in the roof to let out the
> smoke. ... one or two little sleeping berths close to the
> fire, a stone ledge for a candle end, a bag of meal within
> reach for the stirabout and an iron pot which cooks
> food for man and beast... The stone walls of the
> building are several feet thick[9]

Accounts of the lifestyle of sixteenth-century Gaelic Irish
chieftains were recorded mainly by English military
commanders during the turbulent decades of the second half
of the century. Their portrayal of the customs of the country
and people they were sent to conquer, and which differed

from those pertaining to England, is not suprisingly unflattering and biased. Some non-military English travellers, however, were somewhat more objective in their observations. Recording a visit to a chieftain's castle, one wrote.

> The lady of the house meets you with her train.... Salutations past, you shall be presented with all the drinks in the house, first the ordinary beer, then aquavitae, then sack, then old ale...The fire is prepared in the middle of the hall....the table is spread and plentifully furnished with [a] variety of meats, but ill cooked and without sauce....They feast together with great jollity and healths around...the harper begins to tune and singeth Irish rhymes of ancient making.[10]

The main meal of the day was taken at evening. For the landless majority, a porridge made of oatmeal and milk, flavoured with butter or honey and oaten griddle cakes was the staple diet. For the noble classes the diet was plentiful and varied. Beef, mutton, venison, poultry and game were widely consumed with vegetables such as cabbage, onions, wild garlic, watercress and leeks. Salmon, herring and shellfish were an added luxury to the diet of those with access to rivers and to the sea. Dillisk eaten with butter was considered a delicacy. Meat was generally boiled or roasted on a spit *bir*. Buttermilk was a favourite drink of all classes and was 'wonderfully cold and pleaseing',[11] according to one description. Native *uisce beatha* or whiskey, ale and great quantities of wine from France and Spain, were widely consumed. Mead, a honey-based drink, was considered a special beverage and the area that produced it praiseworthy. O'Malley's territory of Umhall, particularly in the vicinity of Murrisk, was notable for mead, as the old laudatory expression, 'mead-abounding Murrisk' acknowledges. Meals were served in the chieftain's house on

low wooden trestle tables. Meat was placed on large wooden
or pewter platters from which everyone helped themselves by
cutting slivers with a knife. Food was eaten with knife and
hands, forks were still a rarity.

In summer, like his contemporaries, Dubhdara O'Malley
and his household left Belclare to go 'booleying', to graze
the clan cattle herds in the mountain uplands, where they
lived in temporary accommodation. This custom had its
origins in the Celtic past and survived in O'Malley territory
until recent times when

> grazing in common was lately found by the Congested
> Districts Board, in full operation on Clare island and in
> re-arranging the land there they wisely left the old
> cutom undisturbed'.[12]

In the seventeenth century, an English traveller, John
Dunton, while on a visit to Granuaile's grandson,
Murrough-na-Mart O'Flaherty in Connemara, described
the lifestyle of a chieftain during such a booley.

> The house was one entire long roome without any
> partition In the middle of it was the fireplace with a
> large wood  fire which was no way unpleaseing tho in
> summer time. It had no chimney but a vent hole for the
> smoake at the  ridge.

He was told by the O'Flaherty chieftain

> That they had newly put up this for a 'booley' or
> summer habitation, the proper dwelling or mansion
> house being some miles farther neare the sea, and such
> a one they commonly built everie yeare in some one
> place or other, and thatched it with rushes. I had sheets
> and soft white blankets...and they assur'd me no man

ever gott cold lyeing on the green rushes, which indeed
are sweet and cleane, being changed everie day if rain
hinders not.

Dunton was entertained by O'Flaherty during his stay

> We had at dinner no less than a whole beef boyl'd and
> roasted, and what mutton I know not so profewsly did
> they lay it on the table. At the end where the lady sate
> was placed an heap of oaten cakes above a foot high, such
> another in the middle and the like at the lower end, at
> each side of the middle heap were placed two large
> vessels filled with Troandor or the whey with buttermilk
> and sweet milk...We had such ale...and bulcaan, and
> after dinner myn host ordered his doggs to be gotten
> ready to hunt the stagg. He had his horse saddled and
> one for me too... Eighteen long greyhounds and above
> thirty footemen made up the company.[13]

Such a lifestyle was redolent of the ancient sagas of the
Celtic world from where it was derived.

Cattle were the principal source of wealth of the Gaelic
clans and hides a major export. Fishing was the main source
of income for the O'Malleys and the building and
maintenance of the clan's fleet of fishing and trading vessels,
nets and other fishing equipment was an essential part of
clan work. Leisure time was spent hunting the red deer
which abounded in the Umhalls, with the help of the Irish
wolfhound, and also the ferocious wild boar which was the
emblem on the O'Malley shield. Falconry was another
favourite activity of the Gaelic chieftains and the best
falconries were to be found in west Connaught. Travelling
storytellers and musicians entertained the chieftain's
household during the winter months. These itinerant

entertainers were also an essential source of news and gossip. Chess, dice and card-playing were popular pastimes and professional gamblers known as 'carrows' *gearbhach* toured the countryside and were eagerly received in the houses of the aristocracy.

Such was the state of Ireland at the time of Granuaile's birth, circa 1530. The prevailing ethos, language, laws, customs and dress were Gaelic. The power of the Gaelic chieftains and gaelicised Anglo–Norman lords was at its highest. England's authority, with the exception of Dublin and the Pale, had long ceased to have effect on the daily lives of the majority of the people. Yet the reversal of English power had not been translated into political gain by the Gaelic chieftains. For the greater part of the century Ireland remained devoid of any unifying ideological stimulus. A state of disunity and fragmented loyalties prevailed and energy and intellect was wasted on petty power struggles. In sixteenth-century Ireland, tribal warfare, cattle-raiding and blood money were as much part of daily life as they were in the time of Queen Maeve and Cuchulainn. This situation contrasted sharply with most of Europe and more lately with Ireland's nearest neighbour England, where the yearning for change, discovery, knowledge and the achievements of the Renaissance and Reformation permeated and animated and where one centralized authority commanded the allegiance of all.

Such was the antique society that bore and bred Granuaile, a society which, unless it adapted to the fundamental changes which had occurred in the world outside its own orbit, was destined to perish. Like her society Granuaile, in her role as a woman warrior leader, was also a product of the past. She too would have to adapt or pay the price of infexibility.

# CHAPTER THREE

# Fortuna Favet Fortibus

(O'Flaherty Clan Motto)

Granuaile's childhood, like Gaelic children generally, is undocumented. From the meagre information relating to children in Ireland in the sixteenth century we know that the period of childhood was short-lived. The custom of fosterage, widespread among the Gaelic aristocracy, dictated that their sons left the home of their natural parents as early as six years of age. Since succession to the chieftaincy was by the selection of the fittest, their education centred, like their Celtic forebears, on mastering the skills and techniques of warfare, the use of weaponry, riding stirrupless on horseback and proving their mettle as potential chieftains by raiding their neighbours. Such concentration on physical prowess might well have been at the expense of learning. Judging by the crosses made in lieu of signatures on many official state documents of the period, it is clear that many chieftains were illiterate. This fact, however, must be balanced by the existence in the households of most of the prominent chieftains of scribes, lawyers and *filí*, whose function was to provide the chieftain with the necessary written and verbal skills and advice on the administration of his lordship.

While knowledge of the rearing and education of boys in sixteenth century Gaelic Ireland is vague, that of the daughters of the aristocracy is virtually unknown. As in the case of political power, women's access to the bardic ranks was no longer permitted. The days of the female bard and poetess, of the fabled Liadán and Feidelm, were no more. Like the chieftaincy, the honoured ranks of the *fili* were confined to men. The all-male administered bardic, monastic, and the secular post-Norman schools, had no place for female pupils. The scanty records of the few nunneries established in Ireland provide no evidence of any great female scholarship. Yet some Gaelic women, usually the daughters, wives or concubines of the chieftains and the learned classes, despite the educational bias and oftentimes derogatory denounciations of their male counterparts, managed to circumvent the system and become more learned than their menfolk. From the letters of such contemporary Irish noblewomen as Eleanor Butler, Countess of Desmond and Joan Butler, Countess of Ormond, the handwriting, extensive vocabulary, the well-turned phrases displaying a shrewd and consummate knowledge of the political arena, combined with their ability to negotiate skilfully with the most prominent and astute political minds of the time, is testimony to some degree of a formal education. In terms of such political acumen and negotiating skill, it is clear from her correspondence that Granuaile was on par with her Anglo-Norman sisters. Her extant correspondence, numbering some five petitions to Queen Elizabeth and the Lord Treasurer, Lord Burgley and her fascinating auto-biographical answers in 1593 to the Lord Treasurer's set of eighteen questions, reveal an equally shrewd and knowledgeable mind. From the penmanship of her correspondence, however, it seems unlikely that Granuaile was the actual scribe, but from the evasiveness and political cunning displayed therin, she was undoubtedly their author.

Education in Ireland during the sixteenth century was dispensed in a somewhat haphazard way, confined, as in most European countries, to the religious, aristocratic and merchant classes. The Renaissance influence and the aspirations of the Christian Humanists, such as Erasmus and Thomas More, towards making education available to all levels of the laity and particularly their commitment to the education of women, scarcely touched Ireland. Where it did it was confined to the lordships of the Anglo-Norman magnates, the cities and to the Pale. The wives of the Gaelic chieftains, in the main, immersed themselves in rearing their families and managing their households.

By the mid-1500s, Ireland had long abandoned her claim to be the 'island of saints and scholars'. The great monastic schools of Ireland's golden era, which had attracted scholars from all over Europe, were no more. Unlike other European countries there was no Irish university. A few religious schools, mainly teaching canon law and Latin, were still in existence. The sixteenth century was not a golden era of letters in Ireland. The poets' craft was mainly expended on eulogising and elegising Gaelic chieftains and Anglo-Norman lords. But some schools were maintained by the Gaelic bards *filí* where the intricate metres of Gaelic verse were taught to members of the hereditary bardic families. Much of the bardic teaching was verbally rather than literally transmitted, as were the legal tenets handed down by the brehons. As well as verse-making the bardic schools taught Latin, which would seem to have been understood and in use by clergy and laity alike, a knowledge of the Greek and Roman classics, philosophy, some mathematics and probably reading and writing in Gaelic and Latin, mainly to those sons of the Gaelic aristocracy who had not the means nor the desire to seek education in the universities of England or the Continent.

The evidence that Granuaile received some formal schooling is confined to the extant documentation relating to her petitions and answers to the English Court and to the fact that she is traditionally credited with conversing in Latin in her audience in 1593 with the erudite English queen, Elizabeth I. She may also, however, have been conversant in English, as referenced by Sir Henry Sidney about her meeting and conversation with his son, the famous poet-courtier, Sir Philip Sidney in 1577. Her sea-voyages abroad perhaps also made her conversant in the rudiments of languages such as Spanish, French and Scots Gallic. The source of Granuaile's formal education centred on the two houses of friars maintained by her father at Murrisk and on Clare island.

But given the wholly unorthodox role she was later to adopt, contrary both to law and social convention, and to her undoubted ability and success as a leader by land and by sea for over forty years, it is more likely that the brunt of Granuaile's education was geared where her interest lay, in her father's world of ships, trade politics and power. To achieve even part of what she was accused of by the English administration in Ireland, she had to be accomplished in the skills of seafaring. Her ability to sail her ships to Scotland, England and most likely to Spain and Portugal, rank her among the best sixteenth century mariners. Doubly endowed with O'Malley blood from both her parents seafaring came naturally to her. This aptitude and affinity with the sea, her clan's benefactor in war and in peace, undoubtedly shaped her character and outlook. It is reasonable to assume that she accompanied her father as a young girl on many of his fishing and trading voyages and absorbed his knowledge. And there was much to learn: the tides and currents, the moods of the sea, to become, as O'Dugan wrote, 'a prophet of the weather' like her ancestors, to know when to set sail and when to stay ashore, to know the capability of the ships she sailed, about canvas and hawser, ballast and anchor, to navigate by star and by compass, to learn about the perils of the treacherous Irish coastline, the protruding rocky headlands and hidden reefs. The later threat of English warships out to capture her, or competitors in the piracy trade out to relieve her of her cargo and her life, augmented the hazards. Judging by the success and duration of her career by sea Dubhdara O'Malley surely taught his daughter well. It was perhaps her father's character, authority and even his physical attributes, that drew Granuaile to emulate him in later life, to dress like him, to adopt his lifestyle and in effect to become more like a son than a daughter.

Her choice of career, notwithstanding her family background, was unique for a woman. The sea and seafaring were and has ever tended to be the exclusive domain of men. The nature of the environment, both from a physical and decorous point of view, tended to exclude women. Male moral values prevaded ship life. Swearing, disregard for hygiene, carousing, violence, as well as the sexual difficulty posed by the presence of a female among an all-male crew, made seafaring an unattractive and dangerous option for a woman. Seafaring in the sixteenth century was not for the fainthearted. Conditions aboard were primitive, privacy non-existent. For a women's physique it must have been intolerable. Skin toughened under the barrage of wind and spray, hands hardened and nails split by hawser and canvas, bare feet chafed from the roughly-hewn, swaying decks, sodden woollen trews and linen shirts clinging uncomfortably, cold, unappetising food lodged undigested, the discharge of natural bodily functions lacking the usual privacy. To give birth on a bucking galley on the high seas, as Granuaile did, seems unimaginable. Life aboard ship, on lengthy trade or fishing voyages, could be boring with little but singing and gaming to help relieve the tediousness of long days and nights at sea.

Piracy and plundering by sea were also practised by Granuaile as by her ancestors. In remote coastal areas, far from the watchful eye of authority, piracy tended to flourish. In the sixteenth century, the west coast of Ireland was still far enough removed from English control, as the pirate havens of the West Indies were a century later. Piracy in any climate was a grim and dangerous occupation, the penalty for which was death by hanging. Many of Granuaile's English contemporaries were 'seen off at Wapping Old Stairs', the execution site for pirates on the Thames. Those in the West Indies, who dared to go 'on the account', if caught, breathed their last at Gallows Point, east of the old pirate city of Port Royal in Jamaica. Two of the more notorious female pirates who followed in Granuaile's wake, the Irish-born Ann Bonny and her companion Mary Read, 'pleaded their bellies' at their trial in Jamaica to escape the hangman's noose. To be a woman in command of pirate galleys, as Granuaile was for the space of forty years, demanded a stern but fair hand to keep her crew in control as well as success at her trade of 'maintenance'. To fulfill the basic requirement of piracy, 'no prey, no pay', she had to control the fair sharing out of plunder and above all to be more daring and courageous than any of her men.

There has always been much speculation as to how Grace O'Malley became known mainly through folklore as Granuaile (Gráinne Mhaol, the word 'maol' in Irish meaning bald). It is likely that the name Granuaile is a corrupt amalgam of the Gaelic, Gráinne Uí Mháille or alternatively Gráinne Umhaill (Grace of the Umhalls). There are many anglicised versions of her name contained in the English state papers, including Grany O'Maly, Grany Imallye, Granny Nye Male, Grany O'Mayle, Granie ny Maille, Granny ni Maille, Grany O'Mally, Grayn Ny Mayle, Grane ne Male, Grainy O'Maly, Granee O'Maillie.

Granuaile spent her childhood at the family residences of Belclare and Clare Island. There was little to disturb the traditional way of life pursued by her family. The seasons and the sea dictated the ebb and flow of life in the O'Malley household, as it had done for their ancestors. Fishing and trading voyages, storms, occasional shipwrecks, welcomed, as in all coastal communities, as rewards from the sea, summer booleying and deer hunting, the yearly courtesy visit to and by O'Malley's overlord The MacWilliam, the excitement at the arrival of strolling musicians and mummers and particularly the carrows, were the annual highlights. To judge by contemporary reports, Gaelic chieftains seemed addicted to the carrows which, according to one observer, 'so infected the public meetings of the people and the private houses of the lords...'[1] Grace clearly became as 'infected' as her peers and her gambling skills were later commemorated in a sixteenth-century poem:

> *Gráinne na gcearbhach do creach*
> (Grace of the gamblers he plundered)[2]

This unique Gaelic way of life followed by her clan for centuries was, however, about to face its ultimate challenge. Remote from Dublin, the centre of English power in Ireland, hidden behind a protective screen of wood, forest, bog, cut off by the river Shannon, the O'Malleys, like most western clans, were little concerned about the schemes and plots being hatched far away by an English king. These plans were to be carried to a decisive and bloody conclusion by a daughter he had once spurned but who was destined to become England's greatest monarch and Ireland's most determined conqueror.

The winds of change in Ireland's relationship with her powerful neighbour, England, began to blow more fiercely towards the last decade of the reign of England's turbulent monarch Henry VIII. From 1529 to 1536, the Reformation and his matrimonial problems commanded Henry's attention. The revolt and ruthless extinction of the House of Kildare in 1537, directed the King's gaze across the Irish sea to his neglected lordship. Rather than resort to costly warfare, Henry instead instituted the policy of 'surrender and re-grant' in an attempt to gain control in Ireland. To implement this policy, Henry had himself confirmed 'King of Ireland' instead of 'Lord of Ireland', the title held by previous English monarchs. Thus began the new 'Kingdom of Ireland' which was to last until 1800.

The surrender and re-grant policy was based on a spurious theory that all lands held by the Gaelic and Anglo-Norman lords depended on the crown of England. On submission to the king, the chieftain or lord would receive back his lands, in the king's name, provided he agreed to rule by English law and custom and attend the king's parliament in Dublin. In return each would receive an English title equivalent to his Gaelic status. Throughout 1541 some of the most prominent chieftains and lords submitted to the king's deputy in Dublin. Murrough, chieftain of the great O'Brien clan in Munster, was created Earl of Thomond. In Ulster, The O'Neill, regarded by many as the hereditary king of Ireland, submitted and accepted the title Earl of Tyrone. In Connaught, Ulick Burke, the Upper MacWilliam of Galway, was created Earl of Clanrickard.

Thus started the Tudor conquest of Ireland, by means of a policy of subtle effectiveness. As the chieftains and lords accepted the terms and titles of the English king, so they were obliged to abandon the Brehon laws and customs which had endowed them with their positions of power in the first place. Their acceptance of the terms ran contrary to the Gaelic principles of election and land tenure. Some chieftains felt coerced into acceptance, other did so readily out of greed or disillusionment with the impermanance of the Gaelic system which allowed for little continuity, but most accepted only for so long as it suited their own purpose. It was a triumph for Henry VIII who at his death in 1547 had, by a relatively peaceful and inexpensive, yet effective, policy extended his authority, nominally at least, over Leinster and parts of Ulster, Munster and Connaught. In the remainder of the country, suppression of the native laws and customs, as well as the anglicisation of the native aristocracy, would take longer, but the machinery for their decline had been firmly set in motion.

As yet Mayo remained untouched by the political changes. Up to now the affairs of the country, even of Connaught, were of little consequence to the O'Malley chieftain or his immediate neighbours, provided they were allowed rule their territories unhindered either by Irish or English. In Umhall the fishing was good and O'Malley could afford to thumb his nose at the avaricious merchants of Galway and choose his own markets. The only blip on the scene may have been that his daughter looked set to become the sailor her half-brother Dónal never was. In the male-oriented society of Gaelic Ireland that was something hardly to be countenanced by any father. There was little future for a woman inclined towards male pursuits. The only career move for a woman was towards the marriage bed and for the daughter of a chieftain marriage had also to pay political dividends.

Grace was about sixteen years old when she was married to Dónal O'Flaherty, son of Gilledubh O'Flaherty, chieftain of the Ballinahinch sept, the senior ruling branch, of the extensive O'Flaherty clan. The O'Flahertys were rulers of the vast, rugged territory of Iar-Chonnacht, roughly equivalent to modern-day Connemara. A warlike clan, as their motto 'fortune favours the bold' implies, yet unlike most Gaelic clans of the period, for decades they had co-existed in relative harmony with their neighbours, the O'Malleys, and were allies in war. For Dubhdara O'Malley, politically the match between his daughter and the O'Flaherty chieftain was a satisfactory one. By Gaelic custom, Dónal was the elected *tanaiste* to the senior chieftaincy of all the O'Flaherty septs and in time would rule all Iar-Chonnacht. At the time of his marriage to Granuaile, Dónal was chieftain of the Barony of Ballinahinch. His chief castle was on the coast at Bunowen, some two miles south of Slyne Head, the most westerly point in Connaught. It had a deep harbour with good anchorage and was sheltered by the Hill of Doon. Granuaile's new home was separated from Umhall by the deep fiord of Killary and by some of the most spectacular scenery in the country. It was bounded to the north-west by the Twelve Bens, in the distance southeastwards was the extensive island-strewn waters of Lough Corrib, while all around lay the stones, moors and lakelets of Connemara.

As the daughter of a chieftain, Granuaile did not go empty-handed to her marriage. As was customary in the sixteenth century she brought a substantial dowry *spréidh* to her husband in the form of cattle, horses, sheep and household goods. Special 'sureties for the restitution of the

same', according to Granuaile's own testimony 'in manner
and in form as she hath delivered it', were an integral and
important part of the matrimomial contract, in case of the
death of her husband or, as she testified, 'at other times
they are divorced.'[3] Since divorce was prevalent among the
Gaelic aristocracy, the marriage contracts made provisions
for that eventuality. On the death of her husband or upon
divorce, the wife was entitled to receive in full the dowry she
had brought with her to the marriage. In some parts of
Gaelic Ireland a special tax or imposition *cáin beag* was
raised within the lordship for the maintenance of the
chieftain's wife. On the death of the chieftain, the widow did
not normally receive any part of his property, as Granuaile
later stated, 'the countries of Connaught among the Irishry
never yeilded any thirds to any woman surviving the
chieftain,'[4] which made the imposition of sureties for the
restitution of a woman's dowry such a vital part of the
marriage contract.

Like most young brides, Granuaile might well have
experienced a sense of isolation and homesickness in her
new surroundings. The role expected of her now was that of
wife, homemaker and potential mother, a role at variance
with the independent seafaring career to which she had
become accustomed. To be at the command of her husband,
submissive to him in all things, must surely have been an
anathema to Granuaile. Her upbringing was in an
environment of equality, the sea made no distinction
between female and male sailors. By the later evidence
of her relationship with her second husband, with whom,
the records testify, she was more than a Mrs Mate, it is
difficult to imagine her remaining long in the role of
dutiful wife. Her young husband, as his sobriquet, Dónal-
an-Chogaidh (Dónal of the Battles) suggests, was a

truculent chieftain, hardly a man who would allow his position to be usurped by a wife. A clash of personalities seemed inevitable. But for a time at least, Granuaile fulfilled what society, her father and her husband deemed to be her role. She bore Dónal two sons, Owen and Murrough and a daughter, Margaret, named after her own mother, of whom nothing but her name and ancestry and the fact that she inherited land in her own right in Umhall have been recorded.

However, marriage may have altered Granuaile's way of life but there was little change evident in that of her husband. In 1549 Dónal was implicated in the murder of Walter Fada (Tall) Bourke, son of David Bourke, the *tanaiste* to the MacWilliam of Mayo. The murder was committed at the O'Flaherty castle of Invernan in Moycullen, west of Galway city. It is recorded that Dónal murdered Walter at the instigation of his sister Finola, stepmother of Walter, so that her own son, Richard, might be the sole heir of his father and a step closer to become a future MacWilliam, the most coveted chieftaincy in Mayo. Dónal's likely gain from the murder is less clear. The promise of an alliance between himself and Richard, when as The O'Flaherty and The MacWilliam respectively, together they would control Mayo and Iar-Chonnacht, could have been the incentive. However, only part of the plot was realised while the rest turned out in a way that neither Dónal, Finola and especially Granuaile, could have anticipated.

While her husband continued playing the role of warlord, constantly feuding with his neighbours, particularly the Joyce clan with whom he was in dispute over possession of a castle in Lough Corrib, Granuaile was not content to be a stay-at-home wife. Judging by later records which accuse her of being in action for over forty years, it is clear that what Gaelic law denied her as a woman she simply took for herself. It was during her marriage to Dónal-an-Chogaidh that tradition also holds that, whether through his inadequacies as a chieftain or simply by her own inclination, Granuaile superseded him in his authority over his clan and more incredibly still, was accepted by his clansmen, to such a degree that many of them chose to leave Iar-Chonnacht with her later.

Bunowen castle was an ideal base from which to launch a new chapter in her seafaring activities. Around this time the first reports of her attacks on ships sailing into the busy port of Galway were recorded. Galway city was hostile to the O'Flahertys, about whom the Galway citizens had inscribed over the west gate of the city 'From the ferocious O'Flahertys, Good Lord deliver Us.' Because the corporation of the city imposed taxes on the clans who traded there, Grace and her followers sought to do the same on the seas off their territory. Out of the cover of the coastal islands and bays their galleys swooped on the lumbering merchantmen. Negotiations for safe passage into Galway were rewarded by a toll or part of the cargo. Laden with the agreed or extracted spoil, Granuaile and her men disappeared into some uncharted bay on the indented coastline. The corporation of Galway city was powerless against such attacks and conveyed its frustration to the English Council in Dublin.

The continuing roads used by the O'Malleys and O'Flaherties with their galleys along our coasts, where there have been taken sundry ships and barks bound for this poor town, which they have not only rifled to the utter overthrow of the owners and merchants, but

also have most wickedly murdered divers of young men
to the great terror of such as would willingly traffic...[5]

Whether leadership was forced upon Granuaile out of
necessity or not, there had to be a receptive ambitious need
within her which drove her to take on the mantle of power
at a time and in a society that sought to consign women to a
life of domesticity and dependence. Gaelic society
demanded that their leaders were strong of will and body,
able to protect those who gave them allegiance and to defend
their domain. Any sign of weakness or fraility on the part of
a chieftain was certain to unleash the ambitions of
competitors for his office. To retain control of her crewmen,
to enforce her will, it was essential that Granuaile led by
example, enduring and outdoing the men she lead, by land
and by sea, as a later poem testifies regarding her attack on
the castle of Renvyle.

> No braver seaman took a deck in hurricane or squalls
> Since Grace O'Malley battered down old Currath
> castle walls. [6]

It was undoubtedly her strength of character, charisma,
absolute courage, adaptability and self-belief that propelled
Granuaile into a position of leadership during the most
turbulent decades in the history of her country.

Across the Irish Sea another woman was preparing to
assume the role of leader in a man's world. She was to excel
and be immortalised as the greatest of England's monarchs.
Her impact on Ireland, however, was destined to destroy
forever the society that nurtured and sustained Granuaile.
Elizabeth I assumed the throne in November 1558 and
commenced her long and powerful reign which was to end
with Ireland brought to heel, the might of Spain shattered

and the security of England, the yardstick of her policies, achieved. It was a time of dangerous uncertainty for the young queen who ascended the throne in the knowledge that many of her own subjects, because of her father's divorce and the fact that she was a woman, had reservations to her right. The implementaion of the Reformation provisions became imperative to copperfasten her position, since Catholicism regarded her as illegitimate, without any right to rule. Her rival to the throne, Mary Queen of Scots, had married the Dauphin of Catholic France. The prospect of France and Scotland allied against her was a very likely prospect. Although Elizabeth was no religious bigot, in England fidelity to Catholicism soon became synonymous with disloyalty to her and, as her reign progressed, in Ireland, to rebellion against her.

Initially Elizabeth was to continue her father's policy of surrender and re-grant in a bid to conquer Ireland by civil rather than expensive military means. A parliament was assembled in Dublin in 1560 to establish the new queen's title and to reverse her dead sister's attempt to re-establish the old religion. In Ulster, the new chieftain, Shane O'Neill, resisted all attempts to accept English rule. Because of his strength and the remoteness of his country, Elizabeth had little option but to make peace with him, acknowledge him as The O'Neill and to withdraw the recently established English garrison at Armagh. In Connaught, the Earl of Clanrickard preserved his outward show of loyalty to the Crown and maintained a watching brief on the Mayo Bourkes who under Finola's son, Richard, had hired a force of over one thousand Scots mercenaries to plunder the lands of MacMaurice and Lord Athenry in Galway. Clanrickard eventually defeated them, killing seven hundred of the Bourke army. Richard Bourke escaped back to Mayo where English law had as yet to obtain a footing.

In Iar-Chonnacht, however, the first inkling of the expansion of English power soon manifested itself. In 1564 a minor chieftain of the O'Flaheties, Murrough-na-dTuadh (Murrough of the Battle Axes), chieftain of Gnomore, in the northern part of the Barony of Moycullen, commenced a campaign to extend his power. He attacked the Earl of Thomond, then the Earl of Clanrickard, whom he defeated decisively at Trá Bán (the White Strand), two miles west of Galway city. This incident was too serious to be overlooked by the English authorities. To overcome Murrough by force would prove too costly, given his undoubted strength and the remoteness of his territory. If, however, he could be persuaded to become loyal to the Crown, it would prove an advantage in spreading the anglicisation policy further west. The Queen issued Murrough with a pardon and appointed him lord of all Iar-Chonnacht. In return, Murrough promised, 'to observe the Queen's peace, to appear and answer at all sessions within the province...to satisfy the demands of all the Queen's subjects...'[7] The appointment was a repudiation of Brehon law. Murrough was a minor chieftain in the O'Flaherty hierarchy. There was already an elected chieftain and Granuaile's husband, Dónal-an-Chogaidh, was his *tanaiste*.

This first example of the Elizabethan divide and conquer policy, which was to be used so effectively throughout the century, had the desired effect in weakening Gaelic power and setting native and English law on a collision course from which only one side could emerge the eventual victor. The peace of Iar-Chonnacht was shattered as the scene was set for a renewal of inter-tribal warfare, intrigue and double-dealing as each sept tried to take advantage of the situation. Granuaile's husband, as *tanaiste* elect to the chieftain according to Gaelic law, had most to lose. Granuaile, about to embark on her own career as a leader, watched her husband's status as future chieftain usurped by an outside force which appeared more powerful than the native law which had created him *tanaiste*. As the scramble for power erupted among the O'Flaherty septs, it was clear that the old customs were under threat, and right by Gaelic law, unless it could be enforced by strength, could be simply set aside.

Dónal-an-Chogaidh died soon after these developments. According to tradition, he met his end inevitably at the hands of his traditional enemies, the Joyces, in a revenge attack for taking their island-fortress in Lough Corrib. Because of his inordinate pride and the courage he displayed in defending the castle against them, the Joyces had christened Dónal, *An Cullagh* (The Cock). On his death, with joyful anticipation, the Joyces descended on 'Cock's castle'. They reckoned without Granuaile who, leading her husband's clansmen, defended the castle with such skill and bravery that the castle was quickly renamed, Hen's Castle *Caislean-an-Circa*, the name it retains to this day.

Tradition also holds that some time later, a strong force of English soldiers out of Galway besieged Granuaile and a few followers in Hen's castle. Conditions within grew desperate but Granuaile was determined not to surrender. She had the lead roof of the castle stripped, melted down and the molten liquid tipped over the parapets onto the besiegers, who beat a hasty retreat to the mainland to continue the siege from a safer distance. With no boats to escape, Granuaile despatched one of her men under cover of darkness to the Hill of Doon, to light the beacon there. She had established a network of such beacons as signals of danger. Soon her followers arrived to assist her and lifted the siege of Hen's castle.

Following the death of her husband, Granauile experienced the discriminatory dictates of Gaelic law. Despite her competence, bravery and success as *de facto* chieftain, the law would not countenance a woman chieftain and her husband's cousin was elected to succeed him. Her sons, Owen and Murrough, were young men and inherited, as Granuaile later testified, 'the fourth part of the Barony of Ballinahinse',[8] from their father. They were immediately thrown into the cauldron of unrest that the Queen's appointment of Murrough-na-dTuadh had provoked. After Dónal's death, Murrough-na-Tuadh 'entered into Ballynehinsey...there did build a strong castle and the same with the demain lands thereof kept many years'.[9] Granuaile's son Murrough, by adopting the same tactics as his adversary, Murrough-na-Tuadh, eventually recovered his father's lands and castle of Ballinahinch.

Having tasted power, Granuaile was not likely to be denied by law or social propriety. Taking with her the O'Flaherty men who wished to continue to serve under her, she returned to her father's territory of Umhall and settled on Clare Island. From there with a flotilla of three galleys and a number of smaller 'baggage' boats, she launched herself on a career of piracy and plunder, which she euphemistically later described as 'maintenance by land and sea',[10] a career that was to establish her as the legendary Pirate Queen of Ireland.

*Principal 16th Century Lordships. (Private collection)*

*Right:*
*O'Malley Coat of Arms.*
*(Private collection)*

TERRA·MARIQUE·POTENS·

*Above:*
*Galley shown on 1590*
*Jobson map of Ulster.*

*Right:*
*Impression of*
*Granuaile's Galley.*
*(Illustrated by*
*Monica Kennedy)*

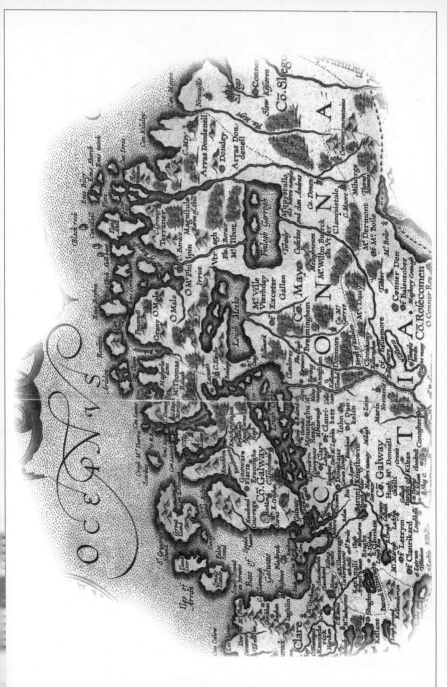

*Boazio Map of Ireland, with Principal Lordships and Chieftains, 1609.*
*(Private collection)*

*Gaelic Chieftain and Kerne. (Derrick, 1581)*

*Galway City, 1611. (Private collection)*

*Chieftain and Entourage, Summer Feasting.* (Derrick, 1581)

*Clare Island Castle. (Dúchas The Heritage Service)*

*Kildawnet Castle. (Dúchas The Heritage Service)*

*Warfare – 16th Century Ireland. (Derrick, 1581)*

*Sir Henry Sidney, English Lord Deputy, leaving Dublin Castle. (Derrick, 1581)*

# Chapter Four

# The Pirate Queen

*There stands a tower by the Atlantic side*
*A grey old tower, by storm and sea-waves beat.*
*Perch'd on a cliff, beneath it yawneth wide*
*A lofty cavern of yore a fit retreat*
*For pirates galleys, atho' now you'll meet*
*Nought but the seal and wild gull, from that cave*
*A hundred steps do upwards lead your feet*
*Unto a lonely chamber. Bold and brave*
*Is he who climbs the stair, all slippery from the wave*

Irish Pedigrees, vol II

As the widow of a chieftain Granuaile was entitled to the
return of her dowry or marriage portion. She was also due to
receive what was known as 'thirds', a percentage of her late
husbands property. But according to her later testimony she
maintained that 'the countries of Connaught among the
Irishry never yielded any thirds to any woman surviving the
chieftain, whose rent was uncertain, for the most part
extorted.'[1] But in view of the action she took on the death of
her second husband, it is unlikely that she left Ballinahinch
emptyhanded. By the early 1560's she had returned to the
O'Malley territory of Umhall, where her father was still
chieftain. As his daughter and, more particularly, as sole heir
to the lands of her mother, Margaret, it made sense to return.
Clare Island with its stark tower-castle was an ideal base for
an aspiring sea-trader and pirate. The castle afforded an
encompassing view of Clew Bay, while its sheltered location
made it virtually indiscernible to passing shipping to the

west. Little could move in or out of the bay without being observed by the inhabitant of Clare Island Castle.

While there is little recorded information relating to Granuaile's activities on her return to Umhall, it is clear that from the outset she was involved in fighting her corner and establishing her authority. In a petition to Queen Elizabeth in 1593 she maintained that circumstances, on which she wisely did not chose to elaborate,

> 'forced her to make head against her neighbours who in like manner constrained your highness fond subject to take arms and by force to maintain herself and her people by sea and land the space of forty years past. [2]

She was also accused in 1593 by an English military governor of being a 'nurse to all rebellions in the province for this forty years,'[3] which would imply that from her early twenties Granuaile was operating as an independent warrior chieftain, fighting her way to power in the whirlpool of Gaelic tribal warfare.

It was during this period of her life that she gathered her force of 'two hundred fighting men' capable of fighting under her leadership in 'Ireland and Scotland'. Her links with Scotland were based on plundering raids but also in the importation of the famed gallowglasses. They were hired, usually from May to September, and Granuaile provided their transport. She prudently ensured a 'back-load' for her galleys on the return trip in September with plunder from the outlying Scottish islands.

Her army comprised men from many clans, such as O'Malley, Bourke, O'Flaherty, MacCormack, MacNally, MacConroy, Clandonnels. That these wild clansmen were prepared to abandon their own clan, pocket their animosity towards each other and, strangest of all, accept the leadership of a woman, contrary to male pride and native mores, is, given the times, an unique tribute to Granuaile. In an age in Ireland where loyalty was transient, especially as England sought to undermine the very foundations of Gaelic Ireland, their allegiance to her lasted until the end. That she was successful at her trade undoubtedly helped maintain their loyalty. We know that she was an active and courageous leader, leading her men personally into battle by land and sea. Long after Granuaile's death, as late as 1627, an English lord deputy recalled her prowess as a warrior leader, that she had 'borne arms…was famous and is yet renowned by them [the people]…'[4]

She is said to have been immensely proud of her followers and to have said 'go mhfearr leí lán loinge de cloinn Conroí agus cloinn MicAnallaidh ná lán loinge d'ór'[5] (that she would rather have a shipful of Conroys and MacNallys than a shipful of gold). That she could offer the English lord deputy an army of two hundred fighting men, willing to fight wherever she commanded, is testimony to her status as a leader of men. That they trusted her capabilities to lead them successfully and safely by land, and especially by sea, was obvious. But to enjoy the loyalty, trust and admiration of her mixed bunch of hardy clansmen and mariners she must also have possessed some special charisma that forged such a lasting bond between them. She undoubtedly enjoyed being in the company of men, of being 'a man's woman', unaffected by female reticence or false modesty in living in close proximity with her men. We know that she indulged in at least one male pursuit – gambling – and folklore maintains that her sexual exploits were in keeping with her seafaring life. Sir Henry Sidney's description of her at their meeting on 1576 as being 'notorious in all the coast of Ireland', perhaps is testimony to this side of her character. It is also hinted in the state documents, that she may have had a son out of wedlock. However it must also be said that sexual promiscuity was often an insidious charge made to demean women who stepped out of what was deemed by society as a woman's place or role. It is also clear from the state papers of the time that Granuaile, like her great contemporary, Queen Elizabeth I, was given to angry outbursts punctuated by swearing.

When her father, Dubhdara, died, most of the O'Malley fleet seems to have come under her leadership. She controlled the passage into Clew Bay, and her O'Malley relations were established at Kildawent, Carrowmore, Cathair-an-Mart, Murrisk and Belclare. Later with Doona Castle in her hands, she commanded the passage north towards Erris and Tirawley. From Donegal to Waterford, all along the Irish coastline, her attacks by sea were numerous and widespread. Her fame grew. Stories of her exploits were peddled from port to port. On land she began to accumulate extensive cattle and horse herds, which later in 1593 numbered, by her own admission, over one thousand head, making her a very wealthy woman indeed.

There are many traditional stories told about her activities at this time, her attacks on various castles along the coast. She demolished part of Curradh Castle at Renvyle with a cannon ball shot from the deck of her ship anchored in the bay. Whenever she alighted on nearby Inishboffin, she impounded the islanders' boats. On the Aran Islands she was not welcomed and, according to one account, when she came with 'her people in ships to Port Mhurbhe [Kilmurvey Bay] the battle raged east to Cill Éinne.'[6] In Burtonport, Killybegs and Lough Swilly, the O'Boyle and MacSweeney clans were subjected to her raids, while her attack on the castle of O'Loughlin in the Burren has passed into legend.

Her seizure of the lonely castle of Doona on the coast of Erris was traditionally said to have been in reprisal for the murder of her lover by its owners, a sept of the MacMahon clan. According to legend, Granuaile was on a pilgrimage at the holy well on Clare Island on St Brigid's Day when news was brought to her that a ship had foundered near Achill Head. The chance of salvage proving stronger than religious observance or foul weather, Granuaile and her men set sail in the teeth of a gale, across the storm-tossed stretch of water that divides Clare Island from Achill. Almost four hundred years later that same crossing was undertaken in a similar storm by the scientist, Robert Lloyd Praeger, who organised the unique scientific survey of the island in 1909. He wrote of the experience:

> Away we went under one scrap of sail, over great waves roaring in from the west. The boat rushed down into deep troughs where there was no breath of wind and only water all round and up again over high crests where the wind half choked us, and we got a momentary wide glimpse over far-stretching angry seas to distant black foam-rimmed cliffs...[7]

On arrival off Achill Head Granuaile found that the ship had broken up. Amidst the wreckage she found a young man caught in the rocks. She took him abroad and brought him back with the salvage to Clare Island. His name was Hugh de Lacy, the son of a wealthy merchant from Wexford. They became lovers, but their joy was short-lived. While hunting deer in Achill, Hugh was killed by the MacMahons of Doona Castle. Heartbroken Granuaile plotted her revenge. Soon afterwards the MacMahons came on a pilgrimage to the nearby holy island of Caher. High on the ramparts of her castle on Clare Island, Granuaile watched and waited until they had landed on the island. Like an eagle she swooped, captured their boats, cutting off their means of escape. She overpowered the MacMahons and killed those responsible for Hugh's death. Her revenge still not assuaged, she sailed for Doona, routed the garrison and took the castle for herself.

Granuaile's determination to avenge a wrong was further demonstrated when a neighbouring chieftain tried to steal her property. She set off in pursuit. The chieftain hid in a church on a small island whose only inhabitant was a holy hermit. Surrounding the church, Granuaile vowed to starve the chieftain into surrender as it was against the custom of sanctuary to capture anyone by force in a church. With the help of the hermit, the chieftain dug a tunnel to the cliff-face, from which he lowered himself with a rope into a boat, and made good his escape. Breaking his vow of silence, the hermit informed Granuaile that her quarry escaped and scolded her for trying to harm someone who had sought sanctuary in his church. Granuaile's reply was unfortunately not recorded.

Perhaps it is her association with Howth Castle in County Dublin that best demonstrates the boldness and daring of Granuaile. Situated some ten miles from Dublin, Howth was then the principal port for the city. Granuaile's ship put in at the port for water and provisions for the journey back to Mayo. As a chieftain in her own right, Granuaile, as was the Gaelic custom, sought hospitality at the castle of the local Earl of Howth, St Lawernce. But Howth was in the English Pale and no such Gaelic customs of automatic hospitality applied. Granuaile found the gates of the castle locked against her and was told that the Lord of Howth was at dinner and would not be disturbed. Furious with such inhospitable treatment Granuaile returned to her ship. On the beach before the castle she met the young grandson of the Lord of Howth. She kidnapped the young boy and sailed away to Clew Bay. On learning of the abduction of his grandson and heir, Lord Howth set off for Mayo, in the hope of securing the release of his grandson from the clutches of such a notorious pirate by payment, as he expected, of a ransom. Scorning his offer of gold and silver, Granualie made St Lawrence revise his definition of hospitality. She extracted a promise from him that the gates of Howth Castle would never again be closed and that an extra place would always be set at his table for anyone seeking his hospitality. Relieved at the simplicity of her request, Lord Howth readily agreed and departed from Mayo with his grandson.

Traditionally the abduction of the heir of Howth has always been ascribed to Granuaile. However, the seventeenth-century historian and genealogist, Duald MacFirbis, in his *Great Book of Genealogies,* maintained that the perpetrator of the deed was Richard Bourke, MacWilliam of Mayo from 1469 to 1479:

> This was the very same Richard who took the Lord of Beann Edair [Howth] and brought him with him to Tirawley, and there was nought else required of him for his ransom but to keep the door of his court open at dinner time.[8]

But MacFirbis's statement must be examined in the light of the treatment and attitude of Irish annalists and historians in general to Granuaile. While the English state papers and associated manuscripts of the period include numerous references to her and her extraordinary career, her exclusion from contemporary Irish annals and histories shows a remarkable bias. When put in the context of Granuaile's actions and unorthodox life, the bias is perhaps more easily understood. To later generations of historians and annalists, Granuaile simply did not fit the required mould, as an Irish patriot and as a suitable example of Irish womanhood. To eliminate rather than to explain her was perhaps the easier course for their nationalistic and often religious authors, and in this regard MacFirbis was no different from his contemporaries.

Tradition is steadfast in its assertion that it was Granuaile who abducted the heir of Howth, and Grace O'Malley's name is commemorated on the street signs in the village today. At Howth Castle, which is still in the ownership of the St Lawrence family, to honour her agreement made with their sixteenth-century ancestor, an extra place is always set at the table and the old gates are never closed. Records in the keeping of the family, further testify to her association with the incident.

They state that:

> Lord Howth gave a ring to Grace O'Malley as a pledge on the agreement… it was preserved in the O'Malley family until in 1795, when an Elizabeth O'Malley married John Irwin of Camlin, county Roscommon, when the ring moved to the Irwin family. An Irwin son emigrated to America taking the ring with him. He was a solicitor and married and later his grandson, John Vesberg, a New York solicitor, had it mounted into a brooch.[9]

The abduction incident is furthermore so much in keeping with Granuaile's style and character that as E. Ball recorded in his book, *Howth and it's Owners*, 'the possibility that an incident such as tradition relates may have occurred is beyond dispute.'[10]

While Granuaile received short shrift from Irish historians and annalists, tradition and folklore more than compensated in keeping her memory alive. Many of the stories relating to her have been preserved by word of mouth, handed down from one generation to the next. In 1838, the famous scholar, John O'Donovan, when collecting information for the Ordnance Survey letters relating to Co. Mayo, found that Granuaile was then

> most vividly remembered by tradition and people were living in the last generation who conversed with people who knew her personally. Charles Cormick of Erris, now 74 years and six weeks old, saw and conversed with Elizabeth O'Donnell of Newton within the Mullet, who died about 65years ago who had seen and intimately known a Mr Walsh who remembered Gráinne. Walsh died at the age of 107 and his father was the same age as Gráinne.[11]

These folk stories and legends are in themselves a tribute to Granuaile, an acknowledgement of the impact she made on her time and on the community in which she lived.

As Granuaile continued to pursue her trade by land and sea from her base on Clare Island, political events outside her domain and outside Ireland slowly began to impinge on the freedom both she and her Gaelic world enjoyed. In Europe, religious polarisation between Catholicism and various branches of Protestantism erupted in France into a fierce and bloody struggle for religious supremacy. King Philip of Spain, self-appointed defender of the old religion, was determined that Protestantism would not gain a foothold in Spanish-contolled Netherlands. The Protestants of the Netherlands looked to Queen Elizabeth for help, which she promised, thus setting England on a collision course with Spain.

In Ireland, an on-going feud between two powerful magnates, the earls of Desmond and Ormond, exploded into war. In a pitched battle at Affane in 1565, Ormond defeated Desmond. The incident brought the unstable political situation in Ireland, and its potential to be used as a weapon against England by Spain, into focus. But money or lack of it, as ever, blunted England's resolve and ability to conquer her neighbour.

However, when the queen's deputy in Ireland began to write about the possibility of colonisation as a means of extending England's hold over its neighbouring island, an effective and less expensive possibility of bringing Ireland to heel presented itself. It was one that was to have a profound effect on the Gaelic world of Granuaile and her contemporaries, the repercussions of which have lasted to the present day.

The colonisation project was greeted with enthusiasm in England, where younger sons of the landed gentry, with little prospects, given the law of primogeniture, and enterprising adventures from the West Country, saw it as a means to their fortune. First into the fray was Sir Peter Carew, armed with a spurious claim to lands in Meath and Carlow and to Desmond lands in Kerry and Cork. The claim originated in the dim and distant Anglo-Norman conquest four hundred years previously. However, in his enthusiasm to endow himself with the lands and property of Irish chiefs and lords, Carew also laid claim to lands owned by the brothers of the normally loyal Earl of Ormond. This resulted for a time in an unlikely alliance between the rival house of Desmond and Ormond, as they revolted to protect their properties against Carew's claim. But they could not stop the tide and, on the strength of Carew's initial success, scores of his fellow countrymen set their sights on the rich land of Munster, and a mission of land-grabbing on a grand scale commenced. Acquisition and exploitation had to be justified. In the manner and the language of the day, to these pirate-adventurers, Ireland was as remote and unknown as the far-off Americas, peopled by a race as alien as the red-skinned Indians, governed by barbarian chieftains and uncouth brehons and bards – a race and country which would surely benefit from the 'civilising' hand of the superior conqueror. The conquest of Ireland by the English was set in motion.

In Connaught, English authority was further extended in 1569 by the appointment of Sir Edward Fitton as military governor of the province, and by the establishment of a council, consisting of a justice, a provost-marshall, an attorney and sheriffs. The powers of the governor, who was also president of the council, were great, and he in effect exercised the power of the lord deputy in the area. At the same time Sir John Perrot was appointed President of Munster. The presidencies of Connaught and Munster provided the English government with an institutionalised vehicle from whence would emanate legislative policies and military strategies to undermine the foundation and institutions of native Irish law and society, as well as protect the colonisation process. Although the presidency would meet stiff opposition from native power, it was bound to succeed in the long term. By the very institutional aspect of its power, it had the in-built ability to survive the challenge of the divided and individualistic native society it had come to conquer.

In Mayo, native opposition to the newly established English presidency did not take long to materialise.

Governor Fitton and his ally, the Earl of Clanrickard, clashed with the MacWilliam of Mayo at Shrule on the borders of Mayo and Galway. The Mac William was aided by the O'Flaherties and by Richard Bourke, the chieftain of the sept of Ulick of Burrishowle. Both sides claimed victory, but later in the same year the MacWilliam submitted to Fitton and agreed to pay the crown a yearly rent of 200 marks. His death at the end of 1570 marked a milestone in the history of Mayo: during his reign as the MacWilliam, English authority had gained a foothold in an area that had hitherto been a bastion of Gaelic law and custom. It was the start of a turbulent transfer of power from the native chieftains to the English crown that was to continue for a period of some thirty years. As the chieftains saw their power and ancient privileges threatened by the establishment and extension of the new administration, they sought either to oppose the English, if they were strong enough, or to ally with them, if it proved to their advantage.

Granuaile's emergence as a leader in her own right, contrary to both native and English law, coincided with these radical political developments. In many ways there is a curious analogy between Granuaile's struggle, in both the political and personal sense, and the struggle of Gaelic Ireland against Elizabethan England. At first, both are boldly defiant in the face of English encroachment. However, eventually, in the face of the relentless pressure exerted by the English, and the inability of the leaders of Gaelic Ireland to formulate a cohesive campaign of opposition, Granuaile's struggle to maintain her power becomes, like that of the Gaelic world into which she was born, a struggle for survival against the odds.

CHAPTER FIVE

# 'A Most Famous Feminine Sea Captain'

By 1567, Granuaile had relinquished her status of widowhood to marry again. She was now in her late thirties. Average life expectancy for sixteenth-century women was about forty years. Given the dangerous career path she had chosen, it could be said that she was lucky to have survived until then. Traditionally it was held that her second marriage was motivated by material rather than emotional needs, possession of her husband's strategically situated castle of Carraigahowley (Rockfleet) being her principal objective. No doubt her choice of mate was influenced by the fact that his lands had access to many sheltered harbours, including that of Burrishoole, where, according to a contemporary account, 'a shypp of 500 tonnes may lye at ancure at loe water'.[1]

It is quite likely that unlike her first marriage, this time she did the choosing. Her husband was Richard Bourke, chieftain of the sept of Ulick of Burrishoole and Carra, a senior branch of the Mayo Bourke dynasty. His father, David, had been the MacWilliam until his death in 1558. (Richard was stepbrother to Walter 'Fada' Bourke, who had been murdered by Granuaile's first husband, Dónal-an-Chogaidh O'Flaherty.) Richard's prospects in the Gaelic power stakes was undoubtedly another attraction for

63

Granuaile. As chieftain of the sept Ulick and as son of a former MacWilliam, Richard was eligible for election to the MacWilliamship, whenever the coveted title became vacant. His territory in Umhall Iochtarach stretched along the northern shore of Clew Bay, between Achill and Westport. This was not the first O'Malley – Bourke marriage. In the fifteenth century, Granuaile's namesake, Gráinne Uí Máille, had married Thomas Bourke from Burrishoole. Their commemorative silver-gilt chalice is now in the National Museum of Ireland.

Richard's nickname of *'an iarainn'* [iron] was traditionally held to have originated from his habit of wearing an outdated suit of armour inherited from his de Burgo Anglo-Norman ancestors. It is more likely that his name derived from the iron works on his lands at Furnace in Burrishoole.

From the extant records it appears that Richard-an-Iarainn had been married previously or was the father of illegitimate sons. Besides the son he had with Granuaile, three other sons, Edmund, Walter and John, and a daughter Catherine, are named as his in the English state papers of the period. In her correspondence with the English authorities, Granuaile mentions having only three sons. Her son by Richard-an-Iarainn, in a bill of chancery later claimed to be his mother's sole heir. However, Edmund Bourke, in particular, was often mistakenly referred to by the English authorities as Granuaile's natural son. There are some extant documents relating to Richard-an-Iarainn, in both the state papers and in the Westport House manuscript collection (now in the National Library of Ireland). From these it appears that, in common with the majority of Gaelic chieftains of this period, he could not write his name but signed the documents with a cross.

Whatever about his educational shortcomings, Richard

was not lacking in the warlike qualities and battle skills necessary to make him a prominent chieftain and a contender for overall power in Mayo. As early as 1553 he was involved in a tribal dispute with the Bourkes of Gallen who defeated him, took him prisoner and killed 150 of his men. In 1558, when his father was the MacWilliam, in an ongoing feud with the Earl of Clanrickard, Richard-an-Iarainn, with a huge army of 1,200 Scots mercenaries, plundered the lands of MacMaurice and Lord Atherny, allies of Clanrickard, in county Galway. Later, in a fixed battle with Clanrickard, he was defeated with the loss of over 700 of his mercenaries. By the time of his marriage to Granuaile, Richard-an-Iarainn had established himself, both by birthright and by might, as a future candidate for the MacWilliamship, the highest office of power in Mayo and second in the province of Connaught to Clanrickard.

Tradition holds that Granuaile married her second husband strictly on her own terms, opting for a trial marriage for a period of one year. If either of them wished to withdraw from the arrangement after that time, they were free to do so. Trial marriage was much in vogue among the Gaelic aristocracy, and divorce within the Brehon legal system was accepted and availed of by both women and men. As one historian has written:

> In no field of life was Ireland's apartness from the mainstream of European society so marked as in that of marriage…. Down to the end of the old order in 1603, what could be called Celtic secular marriage remained the norm in Ireland…Christian matrimony was no more than the rare exception, grafted onto this system.[2]

Tradition further holds that when their marriage had reached the year's duration, and when Granuaile had

installed her followers in Carraigahowley, she locked her
husband out of his castle, and from the ramparts shouted
down the words of divorce, 'Richard Bourke, I dismiss you',
thereby at one fell swoop acquiring a castle and ridding
herself of a husband. Their divorce was, however, a
temporary aberration. Granuaile and Richard-an-Iarainn
feature together as husband and wife and there are many
references to them in the state papers of the period.

Richard-an-Iarainn's principal castle was at Burrishoole in
Umhall Iochtarach. He possessed another near the present
town of Newport and also the castle of Carraigahowley, the
castle most associated with Granuaile. Situated on a quiet
inlet of Clew Bay, Carraigahowley is a typical square tower
keep of the period. In the time of Granuaile the entrance was
protected by a small barbican. It is some fifty-six feet high,
comprising four stories, linked from the first-floor level by a
spiral stairway, and is surmounted by ramparts and a wall
walk. The lower levels are dimly lit by loop windows and
include some curious features still extant, such as a stone
privy with an outflow down a shaft to the sea, which at high
tide encircles three sides of the castle. The main apartment is
on the fourth floor and was undoubtedly inhabited by
Granuaile on an almost continuous basis until her death. It
has a bright and airy aspect and commands a fine view
towards the sea. It has a flagged floor, a fireplace, recessed
windows and a curious arched doorway on the east wall with
a fifty-foot drop below. This has a less sinister use than one
might suspect, being a loading bay through which objects that
were too bulky to be carried via the spiral stairway were
hauled up by a pulley. In the south-facing wall there is a
loophole through which traditionally it was believed the
hawser of Granuaile's favourite galley was attached to her
bedpost at night. A small stairway leads from this chamber to

the ramparts above. The castle has been partly restored and even in its present stark state it is not difficult to imagine the bare chambers transformed into a comfortable and strategic stronghold.

That Granuaile was the dominant partner in her marriage to Richard-an-Iarainn is evident from the many references to both of them written by the English administrators and military men who crossed their path. At one such meeting it was recorded that Granuaile 'brought with her her husband for she was as well by sea as by land well more than Mrs Mate with him....'[3] Richard-an-Iarainn is usually referred to by the English as 'the husband of Grany O'Maile'.[4] He was undoubtedly a brave chieftain by the standards of the time, and skilled in feats of arms. But his warrior-like attributes seemed ever to be at the expense of political acumen. It was his wife who excelled in this regard. The combination of his strength and her considerable political awareness made them a formidable couple. As was customary, Granuaile brought a dowry with her to the marriage, mainly comprising cattle and horses, for which, as she later recorded, she received from Richard-an-Iarainn 'sureties for the restitution of the same',[5] in case of their divorce or his death.

Their son Theobald was born about 1567. He became more familiarly known in history by his sobriquet, Tibbot-ne-Long *Tibóid-na-Long*, Toby of the Ships. He was said to have been borne on board his mother's ship. De Burgo's *Hibernia Dominicana* acknowledges this theory as the source of his nickname and states, '...bellatorem strenuum et invictum, qui (sc Richardus) ex Grania (aliis Grisella) O'Maly, Dynastae O'Flaherti Vidua, genuit Equitem Theobaldum ny Lung id est, de Navibus quia Mari in Navium Classe natum'[6] ('... the mighty and invincible warrior [that is Richard] had by the widow Grania [alias Grisella] O'Maly of the O'Flaherty family, the knight Theobald ny Lung, that is of the ships, because he was born in a fleet of ships at sea.')

It was also traditionally held that the day after his birth, Granuaile's ship was attacked by Algerian pirates. As the battle raged, her captain came below, where she lay with her new-born son, and begged her to come up on deck so that her presence might rally her men. With the words 'may you be seven times worse off this day twelve months, who cannot do without me for one day',[7] she wrapped a blanket around herself and joined her men. Uttering a ferocious oath she urged them into action, while at the same time she emptied a musket at the Algerians, saying, 'Take this from unconsecrated hands'. The fact that attacks by North African pirates were recorded to have occured on the south and west coasts during at that time lends credence to this traditional account of Tibbot-ne-Long's birth. Her reference to 'unconsecrated hands', refers to a custom in the Catholic church (extant until recent times) that deemed a woman after childbirth unfit to participate in church ceremonies until she went through a cleansing ceremony.

In a poem commissioned from the sixteenth-century poet, Mathgamhain Ó hUiginn, and preserved in manuscript form in the Royal Irish Academy, Granuaile's youngest son is referred to as:

> Tiobóid a Burc of the valiant feats
> Of the hawklike blue eye…
> He is the warrior whose curving neck
> With ringleted golden-yellow hair
> Is secretly loved by girls in every region…
> He is the ruddy-cheeked heir of Gráinne.[8]

It is of interest to note that the poem refers to Tibbot as the heir of his mother and not, as might be deemed more usual, of his father.

Another sixteenth-century poet, the famed Eochaidh Ó hEoghusa, referred to him as:

> Tiobóid, Tower of Achill
> Salmon of Clár Gara
> Emulator of the African Lion....[9]

As was customary, when he was about five years old, Tibbot was fostered by Edmund MacTibbot, a sub-chieftain of his father who resided at Castleleaffy in Burrishoole. Fosterage was an integral part of Gaelic life and was considered an honour by the family chosen as fosters to the son of the chieftain:

> The practice was of considerable political importance, for the person fostered could count on the adherence of his foster family through his life....Conversely, the fosterers would also reap the benefits of support and protection.[10]

Tibbot-ne-Long received the same care, affection and discipline from his foster family as he would from his natural parents. As the son of a chieftain and a future contender in the ruling Bourke hierarchy, his education placed much emphasis on the use of weaponry, such as the sword, javelin and dart, horsemanship and military tactics. He was literate in both Irish and English, as his correspondence with the English administration shows. He possessed a keen and able mind and, as an adult, displayed a far-reaching grasp of both Brehon and English law, which he used to his material advantage. The fact that Tibbot-ne-Long succeed his mother by sea, inheriting her fleet of galleys towards the end of the century, points also to his maritime skills, which undoubtedly were imparted to him by Granuaile.

In 1571, Shane MacOliverus Bourke was elected MacWilliam. Granuaile's husband Richard was elected his *tánaiste.* During his reign, the English administration continued to expand its control over Connaught. In 1574, as a result of a survey undertaken by English officials, Mayo was divided into ten baronies, and the principal clan and chieftains of each barony were listed for the first time. For the barony of Burrishoole it was recorded 'Burris, containing Owle Clan Philbin, Owel Eighter (iochtarach) and Sliocht MacTybbot's lands, Richard-an-Iarainn chief.'[11] In 1575 the English lord deputy, Sir Henry Sidney, paid a second visit to Connaught in an effort to induce the lords and chieftains of the province to surrender their Irish tenures, take back their lands by the queen's patent, rule by English law, and accept sheriffs in their territories. Mayo had managed to stay aloof from the English administrative encroachment, but the day of reckoning had finally arrived. Sidney returned to Galway again in1576 and summoned the principal chieftains of Mayo to appear before him.

Thinking that his power and forces made him immune from the English, MacWilliam at first refused to comply with Sidney's order. The lord deputy then embarked on a divide and conquer policy. He succeeded in luring away MacWilliam's Clandonnell gallowglass, the basis of his power. With MacWilliam thus weakened, Sidney sent the elderly Dean of Christchurch, a member of the Connaught Council, to MacWilliam who now had little option but to submit. Together with his sub-lords of Mayo, including the new O'Malley chieftain, he went to Galway. Sidney recorded his encounter with MacWilliam – 'I found

MacWilliam very sensible, though wanting the English tongue, yet understanding the Latin, a lover of Quiet and Civility'[12] – who impressed him with, as Sidney claims, his desire 'to hold his Lands of the Queen and suppress Irish Extortion and to expulse the Scots, who swarm in those quarters'. The result of MacWilliam's submission was that he agreed to rule by right of English law, to pay two hundred and fifty pounds per annum in rent to the crown and to furnish the English governor with a force of two hundred soldiers for two months each year. In return, Sidney conferred on MacWilliam 'his country…by way of Seneschalship….The order of Knighthood I bestowed upon him…and some other little trifles…', including the imposition of a sheriff on his territory! MacWilliam left Mayo to meet with the queen's deputy as an independent Gaelic chieftain, and returned an indentured English knight. Later, MacWilliam obtained a promise from the English to be created an earl, but it was contended that as he 'had no certain estate in land',[13] the promise was not fulfilled.

MacWilliam's submission had fundamental repercussions for his *tánaiste*, Richard-an-Iarainn who, alone of the Mayo chieftains, had not accompanied him to Galway. It demonstrated that the English were now more powerful than the strongest Gaelic chieftain. It undermined the age-old custom of clientship, the pillar upon which Gaelic power rested, and revealed its inherent weakness when faced with a stronger and united force. It was Granuaile who, more than her husband, realised the implications of MacWilliam's submission and prepared to do something about the situation. By English law, MacWilliam's eldest blood relation would now succeed him, not his *tánaiste*, Richard-an-Iarainn. Granuaile had first-hand experience of how her first husband, Dónal-an-Chogaidh O'Flaherty, had been set aside as *tánaiste* by a stronger usurper who, regardless of legal right by Irish law, had induced the English to support him. Perhaps this was the reason for her decision to make a show of power to the English to let them know that she and Richard were no pushovers.

On his return to Galway in March 1577 to quell a rebellion by the sons of the Earl of Clancrikard, Lord Deputy Sidney, accompanied by his son, the famous poet, courtier and soldier Sir Philip Sidney, met with a most unusual leader, as he recorded:

> There came to mee also a most famous femynyne sea capten called Grany Imallye, and offred her service unto me, wheresoever I woulde command her, with three gallyes and two hundred fightinge men, either in Ireland or Scotland, she brought with her her husband, for she was as well by sea as by land well more than Mrs Mate with him. He was of the Nether Burkes and now as I here (1582) Mackwilliam Euter and called by nickname Richard in Iron. This was a notorious woman in all the costes of Ireland....[14]

Granuaile's plan had the desired effect. Obviously impressed, Sidney noted her sea and military power, and no doubt was glad to accept her offer of assistance, given that his own army hardly numbered much more than hers. Anxious to view from the sea-side the defensive walls of Galway city, which, as he wrote, he found much decayed, he prevailed upon Granuaile to take him out on the bay in one of her galleys. But business being business, Granuaile demanded and was paid for the service by the lord deputy, a receipt for the payment Sidney meticulously later recorded.

His son Sir Philip Sidney had recently arrived in Ireland with his friend, the Earl of Essex, who had been appointed earl marshal by the queen. He had journeyed on from Dublin to Galway to meet with his father. Sir Philip Sidney was captivated by Granuaile and, as his father reported to the queen's secretary, Sir Francis Walsingham, 'This woman did Sr Philip Sydney see and speake withal, he can more at large enforme you of her.'[15] What common ground the middle-aged feminine sea pirate and the sophisticated young Elizabethan courtier found we will never know. That Philip Sidney had recently become a patron of the explorer Martin Frobisher, who was preparing for another voyage to find the fabled North West Passage, perhaps gave them some topic of mutual interest.

Granuaile's submission to the English lord deputy in Galway was no more than a judicious gesture designed to enhance her husband's future claim to the MacWilliamship by, on the one hand, currying favour with the English, and, more especially, by demonstrating her undoubted power on the other. There was to be no change, however, in her activities on her return to Mayo. A few weeks after her meeting with Sydney, she set off south in her ships on a plundering mission to the rich lands of the Earl of Desmond in Munster. The mission did not work out quite as she had planned. She was captured and hauled before the Earl at his great castle at Askeaton. Desmond at this time was fighting for his political survival. The largest and most powerful independent lord in Ireland at the time, he was being pressurised by forces within his own family, who wanted him to preserve the status quo, and by external powers who wanted to make him the symbolic leader of the growing Counter-Reformation movement with its Papal and Spanish backers. At the same time he was being baited by land-hungry Puritan elements in the English administration who saw in Desmond's inflexibility and his vast acres the means of making their fortunes. The indecisive Earl was playing for time. Under suspicion by Queen Elizabeth – recently excommunicated by the pope – of being implicated in a European Catholic crusade against her, Desmond badly needed a reprieve. Granuaile provided him with the opportune token to appease the queen's suspicions. The Earl had Granuaile imprisoned in Limerick gaol.

Confinement for Granuaile, who throughout her life never allowed herself be bound by social or political convention, the essence of whose life by sea was freedom, must have been a living death. Limerick gaol was only the start of her long confinement. In March 1578, when the English President of Munster, Lord Justice Drury, came to Askeaton demanding proof of the Earl's loyalty, Desmond produced his notorious prisoner. Drury communicated news of Granuaile's capture to Sidney in Dublin, describing her as:

> Grany O'Mayle a woman that hath impudently passed the part of womanhood and been a great spoiler and chief commander and director of thieves and murderers at sea to spoil this province....[16]

In a letter to Sir Francis Walsingham at the English Court he writes how Desmond 'sent in also unto me Granny Nye Male one of power and force',[17] as a demonstration of his loyalty. The Queen's Privy Council was suitably impressed:

> We pray you also to signify unto the Earle of Desmond in howe good parte her Majestie and we take it to understand of his so good and dewytfull behaviour, in making soche demonstration of his loyaltie, as you wryte of not only in words but also ... sending unto you Grany O'Mayle and other notorious offenders of his countrie.[18]

Drury ordered that Granuaile be transferred from Limerick to prison in Dublin Castle. On 7 November 1578, having endured imprisonment in Limerick for almost a year and a half, she was taken in chains across the country. Drury met her and her escort at Leighlin in Co. Carlow. He informed the Privy Council:

> To that place was brought unto me Granie ny Maille, a woman of the province of Connaught, governing a Country of the Oflaherties, famous for her stoutenes of courage and person, and for some sundry exploits done at sea. She was taken by the Earle of Desmond a year and a half agoe and hath remained partly with him and partly in Her Matir' gaole of Limerick, and was sent for now by me to come to Dublin....[19]

Drury's inaccurate assertion that Granuaile governed a 'Country of the O'Flaherties' displays a lack of knowledge of Connaught on the part of the English and also the impact undoubtedly made by Granuaile. That her capture and imprisonment were of such interest to the English administration in Ireland and to the Privy Council in England is testimony also to her importance. Imprisonment in the dungeons of Dublin Castle was reserved for the most notable and politically important prisoners, and convicted inmates detained there were seldom released. Granuaile's three companions imprisoned with her were subsequently executed at the castle. Lost to her people, her husband and children, Granuaile must have despaired of ever being set free again.

Sir Nicholas Malby succeeded Fitton as governor of Connaught. Malby was one of the new breed of Puritan military men sent over to implement a more vigorous campaign against the chieftains and lords who continued to strive to retain their lands and privileges. For men like Malby, the independent posturing of the Gaelic and gaelicised leaders in Ireland, the unstable situation which their individual power struggles created, and their resolute adherence to the spirit, at least, of the old religion, were anathema to their Puritan Tudor minds. They saw in Ireland's disordered state both an opportunity for England's enemies and as a means towards personal advancement and reward for themselves. The methods they employed, particularly in Munster and Connaught had as their twin spurs, zeal and avarice.

Granuaile's release came early in 1579, and the reason for it can only be surmised. Perhaps the tentative peace that had descended on the country contributed. Perhaps the English authorities decided that Granuaile, imprisoned for almost two years, had paid her dues and was no longer a threat. One way or another, she was installed at Carraighowley by March 1579, when she was immediately besieged by a force of soldiers out of Galway. The soldiers were under the command of a Captain Martin and were sent to capture her in reprisal for her attacks on Galway shipping.

> This expedition sailed from Galway on 8 March but so spirited was the defence made by this extraordinary woman that they were obliged to retreat on the 26 of the same month and very narrowly escaped being made prisoner.[20]

The victory undoubtedly augmented Granuaile's reputation as a leader by land as well as by sea. Her husband was still waiting his time to become the next MacWilliam, but with less certainty than he could normally expect. The present MacWilliam had converted into a loyal subject of the crown and had become an ally of the English governor, aiding him in keeping Mayo in order. Richard-an-Iarainn's future looked anything but promising.

On 18 July 1579, however, the peace and the waiting were shattered by a holy thunderclap. It reverberated off the high mountain peaks of Kerry and sent shock waves careering across the country to frighten the English Council in Dublin and make Elizabeth's nightmare, that Spain would try to use Ireland as a backdoor to England – a reality. With a fleet of ships, an army of some six hundred Europeans, a banner blessed by the pope, and the promise of indulgences, James FitzMaurice Fitzgerald, cousin of the Earl of Desmond, came to unite and raise all Ireland in 'holy war'[21] against the 'heretic queen of England'. He appealed to the Gaelic chieftains and to the Earl of Desmond for support. While the indecisive Earl pondered his unenviable position, FitzMaurice was shot in a squabble, and Desmond was goaded, by circumstances over which he had little control, to adopt the unlikely mantel of crusader. Sir Nicholas Malby assumed temporary authority in Munster and, 'fired by puritanical religious zeal',[22] burned and looted his way to the very walls of Askeaton Castle. In November 1579, Desmond was proclaimed a traitor, and the dogs of war were let loose over Munster, which was to be ravaged for four long years.

The Earl of Desmond wrote to the MacWilliam and Richard-an-Iarainn to raise Mayo in support of the crusade. The MacWilliam refused, but Richard-an-Iarainn gathered his Clandonnell gallowglass and, with some septs of the O'Malleys and O'Flahertys, marched into Galway. Once again he plundered the territories of O'Kelly and Lord Athenry as a probable decoy for the Desmond forces to raid Limerick and Kerry. The reason for Richard-an-Iarainn's support for the Desmond rebellion are open to speculation. That he had a reputation for warfare and plunder was by then well established. His hope of becoming the MacWilliam had been reversed by Shane MacOliverus' conversion to English law. While his right to succeed to the MacWilliamship was recognised and supported by the Bourke hierarchy, the English, it seemed, would back MacWilliam's brother as next male heir. Like most of his contemporaries, his discontent spread not from any sense of religious persecution by the English crown, but from the crown's endeavours to take away his powers. He saw in Desmond's rebellion a chance to secure what he considered his right by native law. MacWilliam had thrown in his lot with the Engllish. It was logical that Richard would back their enemy. Granuaile's role in her husband's decision was perhaps contradictory. There was little reason to suppose that she would wish to aid Desmond who had sacrificed her to save his own neck. Yet with her husband's future at stake, perhaps she had more to win than to lose.

In February 1580 Malby returned to Connaught from Munster to oppose Richard-an-Iarainn. With MacWilliam's help, he drove him from Galway into Mayo. As Malby advanced, Richard-an Iarainn's gallowglass began to desert him. When Malby took the castle of Donamona and, as he reported, 'put the ward, both men, women and children to the sword',[23] resistance began to crumble. Richard-an-Iarainn fled with a few followers to Clew Bay. 'The 16th I removed to Ballyknock', Malby recorded, 'whither Gráinne ni Maille and certain of her kinsmen came to me.'[24] With the initiative well and truly lost by her husband, a voluntary submission, rather than a forced one later, made obvious sense to Granuaile. That she still continued as a leader, independent of her husband, is evidenced from Malby's statement, as is the fact that she was by now well accepted as such by him and the other English administrators who came into contact with her. She must have soundly cursed her wayward husband as Malby and his army moved right into the heart of Burrishoole and placed a garrison at the abbey, close to her castle. Richard fled with a few followers to an island in Clew Bay and commenced negotiations with Malby from a distance. Eventually he agreed to come ashore and submit in person, but was prevented by a violent storm which blew for six days. As the situation in Munster deteriorated, Malby was ordered by the new Lord Justice, William Pellam, to report for duty there. Pellam reported to England that 'Sir Nicholas Malbie has put an end to the stire in Connaught by Richard Ineran, husband of Grany O'Maillie.'[25]

Malby arranged that Richard-an-Iarainn's submission should be forwarded to him in Munster.

Signed by his mark, Richard-an-Iarainn's submission was couched in suitably remorseful tones. 'He hath fallen from his dewite towards God and Her Maite...'[26] he declared. But while he might have endured defeat in the field, he did not submit blindly and, most likely under Granuaile's guidance, sought the best deal he could under the circumstances. To regroup his followers, the basis of his power, was his first objective. To this effect he offered to 'call backe his followers with theyre goodes to inhabyte the countrye', at the same time intimating that without them the queen would lose the 'rents and dewties' that were forthcoming from them. So that his authority over his followers would not be diminished, especially in the light of the presence of Malby's soldiers in his territory, he sought the restoration of his right as a chieftain 'to take up suche dewties and demands from tyme to tyme as is dewe upon his followers....'[27] With the Desmond rebellion continuing in Munster, Malby had little option but to agree, and Richard-an-Iarainn returned to Burrishoole.

By the end of 1580, however, Malby, Richard-an-Iarainn and Granuaile were embroiled in another confrontation. The MacWilliam of Mayo died in November, and the succession was claimed by MacWilliam's brother, also named Richard, his heir by English law. This time Richard-an-Iarainn and Granuaile combined to enforce their right to the MacWilliamship. They mustered a huge army, numbering '1,200 gallowglass, 700 Scots, 300 kerne and 200 horesmen',[28] to support his claim. Together with the support of the Mayo chieftains, as well as the dubious support of the Earl of Clanrickard's sons, such an undoubted show of strength spurred the English, already committed in Munster, to act swiftly to defuse the situation. Malby marched into Mayo to meet Richard-an-Iarainn, and after much sword-shaking a deal was struck.

Letters patent from Queen Elizabeth, together with articles of indenture, were signed by Richard-an-Iarainn and the lord deputy, Sir Grey de Wilton, on 16 April 1581. They are written in Latin and confer on:

> Richard Bourke, alias Richard Inyeren Bourke, alias MacWilliam Eoghter Bourke, that he be chief of his clan and seneschal of the feudal tenants and followers of our people and nation and of his own clan's and of his own and their lands and tenements...[29]

The indentures detailed the duties required of him whom, they note rather petulantly as having 'assumed the title and name of MacWilliam Eighter Burke... without permission from her Majestie.'[30] He promised to rule by English law, to obey the queen's representative and to pay 'each year 50 cows or fat marta [bullocks] or in place thereof 250 marks legal money of England at the Michelmas term each year', as well as providing food and lodging for two hundred soldiers for up to forty-two days each year. Most importantly, in the case of Richard-an-Iarainn and Granuaile and their capacity and inclination for the importation of gallowglass, the agreement stipulated that he 'would no longer suffer any Scotts or other rebels or enemies of her Majestie... within the limits of his authority and government.'[31]

This stipulation also fell to Richard-an-Iarainn's advantage. With Malby's help, he drove the Scots mercenaries, numbering over one thousand, whom he had hired to pursue his claim to the MacWilliamship, over the Moy river and out of Mayo, thus saving himself the considerable expense of paying their hire.

The letters patent and indentures (Richard-an-Iarainn's copy is preserved at Westport House) are significant in that they confer on a Gaelic chieftain, often in open rebellion against the English crown, a title Gaelic in origin and outlawed by the self-same authority by whom it was being conferred. Gaelic-sounding clauses such as 'chief of his clan', 'that he may tax, exact and levy', and that he shall have ... profits and commodities which he the said Richard has by right possession in the province of Connaught', all testify to the un-English ethos of the office. English policy to extinguish such Gaelic titles as the MacWilliamship on this occasion had to take a back seat to expediency. Richard-an-Iarainn, with the help of his wife, had displayed his undoubted strength and status in Connaught. If a costly war could be avoided by granting him the coveted title with certain English embellishments – such as a knighthood with which he was conferred in September 1581 – then, for the English, on this occasion, expediency proved the wiser course.

Richard-an-Iarainn was also created MacWilliam in the native age-old manner by his client lords of Mayo at the ancient rath of Rausakeera, near Kilmaine, where MacWilliam chieftains had been invested for generations. By virtue of Gaelic custom, he acquired the extensive territories pertaining to the title: Lough Mask Castle with 3,000 acres, Ballinrobe Castle with 1,000 acres and Kinlough near Shrule with 2,500 acres, together with the demesne lands scattered over the baronies of Kilmaine, Carra and Tirawley. In addition, he received all customary exactions and tributes due to the MacWilliam by his client chieftains in Mayo.

Richard-an-Iarinn had achieved the ultimate office of power with the unlikely acquiescence of both English and Gaelic law. His accession, however, was due in no small part to the intuitiveness and ability of his formidable wife, who gave his more overt methods a double-edge with her sea power and political acumen. With the English and Gaelic system of government clashing headlong, Ireland began to be torn apart. Survival became the spur. Those powerful enough resisted English dominance, while others accepted the changes to such a degree and for as long as necessary. Granuaile and her husband had won the first battle in the struggle for survival in Mayo – a struggle that had only just begun.

# CHAPTER SIX

# 'Nurse to All Rebellions'

On his accession to the MacWilliamship, Richard-an-Iarainn moved his household from Burrishoole inland to Lough Mask Castle, situated on the eastern shore of the lake. Granuaile moved with him, at least temporarily. In October 1582 she is singled out in despatches by Sir Nicholas Malby as having been with her husband at a gathering of the Connaught lords in the governor's residence in Galway:

> The Earl of Thomond, Lord Byrmingham, M'William, Richard M'Oliverus, Walter Burke, Murrough ne Doe O'Flaherty, O'Maddin, M'Morris, M'Davy and many gentlemen and their wives, among them Grany O'Malley is one and thinketh herself to be no small lady...[1]

What Granuaile did to deserve Malby's appendage, 'no small lady' is open to speculation. Perhaps as befitted her new title, 'Lady Bourke', and dressed accordingly, she outshone the opposition, this time in her less accustomed role as socialite.

Her son Tibbot-ne-Long, then about twelve years old, was placed in fosterage with a neighbouring chieftain, MacEvilly in the barony of Carra. The MacEvilly clan (*Mac an Mhilidh*, son of the knight) were descended from the Anglo-Norman de Staunton family, who had come to Mayo with the De Burgos at the time of the invasion. They became chief lords of the barony of Carra and, like their overlords the De Burgos, eventually adopted Irish names and customs. Myles MacEvilly owned the castles of Kinturk, Kilboynell (later Castle Bourke), Castlecarra and Manulla.

A strong local tradition linking Granuaile with the MacEvilly clan, and with Kinturk Castle in particular, survived to present times. Stories relating to her attacks on the castle and her eviction of its legitimate owner, Myles MacEvilly, are numerous. It was also said that she exacted a yearly tribute of 'a bag of meal, a fat pig and an ox'[2], from each family in the district. Her bravery in battle and her contempt for cowardice were portrayed in another story. During one of her assaults on Kinturk Castle, she observed Tibbot-ne-Long lose courage in the heat of the battle, and sneak behind her for safety. Granuaile upbraided her son, saying, 'An ag iaraidh dul i bholach ar mo thóin atá tú, an áit a dtháinig as?' (Are you trying to hide behind my backside, the place you came from?) Stung into action by her words, Tibbot-ne-Long resumed his place by his mother's side.

While folklore may well tend to embellish events and people, in the absence of historical records, it is often the sole vehicle whereby the memory of an event or person is preserved. In the case of Granuaile's connection with Kinturk Castle, a place far removed from her traditional stomping ground around Clew Bay, folklore merely supplemented what historical record had, it seemed, failed to preserve. However, among the original manuscripts until recently preserved in the home of Granuaile's descendent, the Marquess of Sligo in Wesport House, confirmation of Granuaile's connection with the MacEvilly clan is recorded in a somewhat different, but nonetheless fascinating, light. Among the manuscripts is a deed, dated 20 May 1582, and signed (his mark) by 'Myles Mc Breyone alias MacEville, chiefe of his name'.[4] In it Myles MacEvilly grants to Richard-an-Iarainn in trust:

> to the use and behoffe of my foster sonn Thibbot Bourk... the castle and Bawne and ten quarters of land to me belonging of and in Kintourk.... The castle Bawne towne and eight quarters of land of Castlecarry and the four quarters of land of Ballykally. The castle towne and barbikan and foure quarters of lands of Moynulla ... together with all the messuages buildings orchards gardynes moores meddowes feedinge pastures woodes and underwoods watter courses fishinges emollements and other hereditaments....[5]

All this the MacEvilly chieftain conferred on Granuaille's son 'for and in consideration of a certaine some of money... and also for other good causes and consideration... be the connsent of me sonnes and cousins.' While fosterage often commanded extreme degrees of affinity, friendship and indebtedness between Gaelic clans, it is extraordinary that a chieftain would willingly, even in consideration of a 'some of money', grant clan property to a foster son, albeit the son of his overlord. The fear of being dispossessed by outsiders, such as the wave of English adventurers who were making their way into Mayo, the need for the MacWilliam's protection, or relief from financial pressure, may have been contributory factors to MacEvilly's action. While Tibbot-ne-Long did not obtain access to the MacEvilly properties until the close of the century, the deed served as a device by which Granuaile's son eventually became the owner of most of the MacEvilly clan property in the barony of Carra. This included Kinturk Castle, the chief castle, where Tibbot-ne-Long eventually died. The deed was also the basis for the legends relating to Granuaile's attacks on Kinturk. While her son was still a minor on the death of his father in 1583, Granuaile may well have attempted to effect MacEvilly's grant forcibly herself on her son's behalf.

As the MacWilliam, Richard-an-Iarainn had attained his life's ambition. His agreement with the English and the continued presence of a complement of Malby's soldiers in his territory did not deter him or Granuaile from enjoying the traditional benefits and status the MacWilliamship bestowed, or indeed from settling old scores. In May 1582, using Malby's troops under the pretext of collecting the rent due to the crown, Richard-an-Iarainn, in time-honoured tradition, invaded the territory of his rival for the MacWilliamship, Richard MacOliverus. A battle ensued and up to twenty of Richard MacOliverus's followers were slain, including his son. That his incursion was more to do with extracting the traditional tributes relating to the MacWilliamship, than collecting Crown rent was his real motivation. Suspicious of his motives but powerless to stop him, all the English could do was order him 'to give either of his sons, Walter or Edmund,' [6] as a pledge for his future conduct.

Later in January 1583, Richard-an-Iarainn and Granuaile showed a marked reluctance to pay the rent they agreed as part of the deal made with the crown for the MacWilliamship. Malby's collector, Theobald Dillon, wrote to the queen's secretary, Sir Francis Walshingham, about his encounter with them:

> I went ther hence towardes the plas wher M'William was, who met me and his wyfe Grayn Ny Mayle with all their force, and did swer they wolde hav my lyfe for

comyng soo furr into ther countrie and specialie his
wyfe wold fyght with me befor she was half a myle nier
me...[7]

The part played by Granuaile in the affairs of her husband's
office, as well as her fiery and daring disposition, were noted
by Dillon. Their combined military strength made him
think hard about attacking them and also gives an indication
of the size of their army at this time.

I being but a C [100] and fyftie [50] foot men and fyftie
horse-men... they were afar greater in number....[8]

which suggests that their forces were in excess of 150 men.

As aristocratic leaders with pedigrees linking them to
remote kings and warrior chieftains, Gaelic-born leaders like
Granuaile and her husband, would have considered English
petty officials, such as Dillon, no more than servants. To have
to endure the insolence of such brash, avaricious, low-born
officials was anathema to their pride and provoked their anger
almost as much as did the dissolution of their power and
English interference in how they ruled their territory. As part
of the machinery set into motion to undermine, overthrow
and replace a culture and a political system that was foreign
and reprehensible to their English minds, these administrators
and military men, with few exceptions, presented to the
Gaelic chieftains they came to overthrow, the least attractive
and bullying face of English colonialism. As ever, to justify
the conqueror's exploitation of their lands and property,
inferiority and fault had to be shown to be found in the people
and in the customs of the country they had come to conquer.

Refusing to deal with such servitors as Dillon, Granuaile
and her husband would deign to do business only with the
governor:

M'William and Shee came to Sir Nicholas to agree
with hym for 600 marks of areradges [arrears] due
upon ther countrie which they thought never to pay.[9]

Richard-an-Iarainn did not live long to enjoy the fruits of his
hard-won honours as the MacWilliam. On 30 April 1583, he
died, despite the turmoil of his life, of natural causes. The
Four Masters in recording his death described him as:

A plundering, warlike, unquiet and rebellious man,
who had often forced the gap of danger upon his
enemies and upon whom it was frequently forced....[10]

His was the last appointment to the MacWilliamship according to the old Brehon custom of tanistry. Backed by the
English, his rival, Richard MacOliverus, succeeded him to
the title. His appointment was hotly contested by the elders
of Richard-an-Iarainn's more senior sept who took to the
field to contest their right by Brehon law. They were
opposed by the English governor Malby who came with a
large army and spoiled the two Owles and 'burned and
totally destroyed Cathar-na-Mart'.[11] Eventually their
opposition to the appointment abated, but only for a time.

 Despite their personal and at times political differences,
Richard-an-Iarainn was a worthy and suitable consort for
Granuaile. While often forced into playing a supporting role
to her more flamboyant and politic ways, they seem to have
been a well-matched couple who together, as well as in their
individual roles as leaders, made an impact on political
events. Richard-an-Iarainn was content and even
encouraged his wife's unusual role, and his standing in the
male-dominated society of Gaelic Ireland would not appear
to have been diminished by his wife's unorthodox ways. In
an age that was more male-oriented than most, Richard-an-

Iarainn emerges as a man sufficiently liberated from the shackles of misplaced male pride to have acknowledged, encouraged and capitalised in his wife's ability and success.

On the death of her husband, Granuaile, according to her own testimony,

> Gathered together all her own followers and with 1000 head of cows and mares departed and became a dweller in Carrikahowley in Boroswole.[12]

Mindful of what had happened on the death of her first husband, Granuaile quickly established claim to one-third of her second husband's property. She later testified that as the widow of a second husband, Gaelic law did not require the restitution of her dowry, so she simply took the law into her own hands and took over one of her late husband's castles in lieu. Her independence during her marriage to Richard is further reiterated in her statement that she 'gathered together all her *own* followers'. The extent of her wealth at this time is substantial. One thousand head of cattle and mares was no mean fortune in the sixteenth, or indeed, any century. Her youngest son, Tibbot-ne-Long, then almost sixteen, left the fosterage of MacEvilly and entered into his inheritance of his father's estate in nearby Burrishoole, which he shared with his half-brothers, Edmund and Walter. At fifty-three, with a personal army, a fortified castle, a fleet of ships and a small fortune, Granuaile seemed set fair to continue her role as an independent leader.

The English governor of Connaught, Sir Nicholas Malby, died the following year. During the period of his governorship major changes had occurred in the province. During his tenure the English administration had gradually but determinedly extended its influence throughout the province. The introduction of a process of rent-paying, in lieu of privileges, for the chieftains, and the imposition of the contentious issue of 'cess', whereby the chieftains, if they were to remain as such, were forced to maintain a specified number of English soldiers in their territories, was now widespread. Legal sessions by right of English law were being held, and English legal practice was being enforced, especially in the trial and punishment of malefactors. While English law was not practised widely throughout all of the province, Malby had laid the foundations for its future extension. Well might the Irish annalists record his death with the epitaph that 'he placed all Connaught under bondage.'[13] Elsewhere in Ireland at this time, the Desmond rebellion had finally petered out with the slaying of the Earl of Desmond in the woods of Glenageenty, near Tralee, in November 1583. For a short time an exhausted peace descended on the country.

John Browne, the newly-appointed sheriff of Co. Mayo wrote, 'the first Englishe man that in the memory of man hath settled hymselfe to dwelle in the countie of Mayo',[14]. He reported:

> That Connaught standeth on good terms and the people live and keep their goods in more safety and travel with less fear and in less danger than in any other part of Ireland.[15]

But it was an uneasy peace. As the English administration continued to undermine the power and privileges of the native chieftains, repercussions were inevitable as the chieftains fought back. The stalemate was finally confronted, firstly on a legal basis and finally on the battlefield. In 1584 Sir John Perrot was appointed lord deputy, and Sir Richard Bingham became the new governor of Connaught. The appointment of these two men was to prove a milestone in the history of Connaught. Diametrically opposed to each other, on both a personal and political basis, the methods they employed in their dealings with the Connaught chieftains were equally divergent. A policy of conciliation by Perrot contrasted with a policy of the sword by Bingham, which was destined to bring him into direct confrontation with almost every Gaelic leader in Connaught, including, and especially, Granuaile.

Richard Bingham came to Ireland with sound military credentials. Born in Dorset, from his youth he had been trained in military service. He served in Scotland, at the famous Battle of Lepanto against the Turks, in France and in the Netherlands. He was in the army of Grey de Wilton at Smerwick Harbour, when the ragged army which had come to aid the revolt of James FitzMaurice Fitzgerald, was unconditionally slain. He was fifty-six when he was appointed governor of Connaught. Described as 'a man eminent both for spirit and martial knowledge, but of very small stature',[16] his narrow visage, accentuated by a pointed, neatly trimmed beard and dispassionate eyes, proclaimed a narrow and inflexible personality and a zealousness for duty. 'The Irish were never tamed with words but with swords,'[17] was his opinion, and one which he diligently sought to put into practice during his tenure as governor of Connaught.

Bingham's harsh reign must, however, be examined within the context of the conditions and attitudes pertaining. Popular opinion has painted him a villain, the 'Flail of Connaught', the executioner of innocent women and children, and he was. But he was no more cruel than his contemporaries. The brutal methods he employed in subduing Mayo are usually attributed to his individual brand of cruelty instead, as they were the accepted rules of sixteenth-century warfare but reinforced by his own racist attitudes towards the Irish in general. Bingham's singular failing was his inability to adapt English policies to the realities of Gaelic Connaught. It could be said that his thoroughness and inflexibility as an administrator, coupled with a narrow perception of duty, made it impossible for him to convert the Gaelic chieftains to English ways without resorting to force. At the same time, his relative honesty as an official of the crown and his diligence to duty, assured him the ill-will and envy of his fellow administrators.

In Munster the English crown had reaped the high price of the rebellion of Gaelic leaders such as the Earl of Desmond. The ruthless and systematic destruction of the countryside by both sides in the war had resulted in what the poet Edmund Spenser vividly described as 'a most populous and plentiful country suddenly void of man or beast,'[18] and a poor return on the Crown's substantial military expenditure. Rather than repeat the experience of Munster, Elizabeth I was not averse to inducing rather than coercing the chieftains of Connaught to abandon their independent status and clientship power over their sub-chieftains, and adopt English law and customs. Weary of the desultory conflict over succession and privilege, and conscious that time had caught up with the outmoded structures and customs whereby they ruled their lordships, many chieftains were willing to seek title to their position and to their lands by English law.

In 1585, Perrot introduced a formula known as the Composition of Connaught, which sought not only the continuance of the 'surrender and regrant' policy of Henry VIII, but to extend English control over other issues hitherto governed by Gaelic law and custom. It sought to abolish the age-old exactions and tributes paid to the chieftains by their sub-lords, as well as the English levy of 'cess'. In its place, a fixed rent of ten English shillings or one Irish mark on each quarter of tillage and pastureland would be payable to the English crown by the chieftains, and a similar rent payable to the chieftains by their followers. A specified amount of land was to be left rent-free to each chieftain. To eliminate the system of clientship, every chieftain was to be responsible only for his own sept and primogeniture was to replace the native election and tanistry custom.

For the Bourkes of Mayo, the Composition effectively ended the MacWilliamship. While MacWilliams were elected up to the close of the century by various dissatisfied factions, the title never again commanded the same power, prestige and privilege. To the holder of the office by English law, it brought security of tenure and inheritance of the title by his eldest male heir. To those denied access to the title by right of Gaelic law, it provided the focal point for future rebellion against the English. Perhaps hopeful that Tibbot-ne-Long would one day succeed his father to the title, Granuaile must undoubtedly have viewed the Composition of Connaught as a reversal of her son's fortune. Whether through duress or fear, the Composition was duly signed by the principal chieftains in Mayo, including Edmund Bourke of Castlebar, by Gaelc law the *tánaiste* to the MacWilliam.

While Perrot temporised with the Connaught chieftains on a legal front, Sir Richard Bingham's methods of reducing their powers by more confrontational methods, was already stirring up anger and opposition among them. Bingham singled out Granuaile for special treatment. As a deterrent to her obvious potential to oppose him, he captured Tibbot-ne-Long and sent him as a hostage to the house of his brother, George Bingham, then sheriff of Sligo.

There he was kept under restraint for more than a year with the sheriff and his family at Ballymote Castle, which had been confiscated from the chieftain, O'Connor Sligo. It was expressed English policy of the period that the sons of the Gaelic aristocracy in captivity should be educated and be made dress according to English custom, in the hope that they might conform to English ways. It would take more than a brief indoctrination for Tibbot-ne-Long to be transformed from a Gaelic chieftain to an anglicised lord, but the process had been set in motion. During his captivity, he was sufficiently instructed in English ways to learn to speak and write English, a fact commented on by Elizabeth, and evidenced in his letters and dispatches preserved among the Elizabethan state papers.

Around 1584, Tibbot-ne-Long married Maeve O'Connor Sligo – 'Meadhbh of the yellow-gold hair, daughter of Cathal',[19] as a sixteenth-century poet described her. She was the sister of Tibbot-ne-Long's future ally, Sir Dónal O'Connor Sligo. The family was one of the three branches of the royal O'Connor family, once kings of Connaught and High Kings of Ireland. By the sixteenth century they ruled an area corresponding to the present-day county Sligo. Their lordship was strategically situated between Ulster and Connaught. To the north lay the extensive territory of the O'Donnell chieftains of Tirconail, who claimed an overlordship of Sligo. Through alliances with O'Donnell enemies, the O'Connor Sligo constantly sought deliverance from his more powerful neighbour. The most recent alliance had been in 1568 when Maeve's uncle had made an indenture with Queen Elizabeth, which he interpreted as a reaffirmation of his overlordship of Sligo, but which the Crown later claimed was confined merely to the barony of Carbury. That claim was put into effect on the arrival of Sir

Richard Bingham who promptly seized the castle of Ballymote and installed his brother there. Whether Tibbot-ne-Long's marriage to Maeve occurred before or during his captivity in Ballymote Castle is uncertain. If, as is more likely, it occurred prior to Bingham's arrival in Sligo, it would seem that Tobbot-ne-Long's detention was intended to deter Granuaile and the sept Ulick from aiding O'Connor Sligo against Bingham as, in the past, they had been prone to aid him against his traditional enemy, O'Donnell. For Granuaile, the captivity of her son, following on the death of her husband, must have been a severe blow. It was the first of many she was to endure at the hands of Richard Bingham and his relations in Connaught.

While Sir John Perrot was the architect of the Composition of Connaught, its implementation was left to Bingham. In the summer of 1585, he held the first session in Co. Mayo. The Bourkes of sept Ulick refused to attend, and fortified themselves in Hag's Castle in Lough Mask, which Bingham subsequently besieged and demolished. The incident seemed of little significance until later in the year when the MacWilliam of Mayo died and Edmund Bourke of Castlebar claimed the title by right of Gaelic law. Bingham, however, bestowed the bulk of the lands and property pertaining to the title on MacWilliam's eldest son, according to English law. The Bourkes rose in a second rebellion against the Governor. They were joined by their traditional allies – the O'Malleys, Clan Gibbons, the Joyces, Clan Philbin – and secretly by Richard Bourke, known as The Devil's Hook *Deamhan and Chorráin*, chieftain of the Corraun peninsula and married to Granuaile's daughter, Margaret O'Flaherty. They were also joined by Sir Murrough-ne-Doe O'Flaherty of Iar-Connacht. Among the names of the rebels sent by Bingham to Sir Francis

Walshingham is that of Tibbot-ne-Long, who by August 1586 had been released from captivity and had joined the rebellion.

Granuaile's eldest son, Owen O'Flaherty, was married to the daughter of Edmund Bourke of Castlebar. There is no evidence to suggest that he was involved in the rebellion of his father-in-law, save for Bingham's contention that he 'was an open rebel'[20]. It seems more likely that when the governor's brother, captain John Bingham, entered the barony of Ballinahinch in July 1586 in search of booty and cattle to feed his army, in time-honoured tradition, Owen and his followers hid with their herds and belongings on Omey island. Granuaile and Sir Richard Bingham both give varying accounts of what then happened. According to Granuaile's testimony, Captain John Bingham found where Owen was hiding

> And came to the mainland right against the said island calling for victuals, whereupon the said Owen came forth with a number of boats and ferried all the soldiers into the island where they were entertained with the best cheer they had.... The said Owen was apprehended and tied with a rope.... The next night...being fast bound...the said Owen was cruelly murdered having twelve deadly wounds....[21]

In his deposition later when charged with complicity in the killing, Bingham claimed that Owen 'was an open rebel ...being prisoner with the marchall's deputy made his escape and in pursuit was slain because he would not stay and yield himselfe...'[22] – a lame justification, which hardly justified the number and severity of the wounds inflicted on Granuaile's son.

Devastated by the murder of her eldest son, Granuaile

actively supported Tibbot-ne-Long, her stepsons, her son-in-law and her late husband's relations in the revolt against Bingham in Mayo. She prepared to sail to Ulster to bring in Scottish mercenaries. She negotiated with the O'Donnell chieftain in Donegal regarding the details – a fact commented on later by Sir John Perrot when he condemned O'Donnell to the Queen as one 'ready to send aid to any that were evil disposed in your kingdom, as of late he did to Grany ne Male to see if they would make any stirr in Connaught.'[23] Alarmed at the extent of Granuaile's power, influence and with an eye to her extensive cattle and horse herds, Bingham sent his brother, captain John Bingham, to capture her, under the guise, as she later testified, of protecting her. She later gave a vivid account of what occurred:

> She was apprehended and tied with a rope, both she and her followers at that instant were spoiled of their said cattle and of all they ever had besides the same, and brought to Sir Richard who caused a new pair of gallows to be made for her where she thought to end her days. [24]

With Granuaile under lock and key, Bingham set out against her family and relations. He had the Bourke hostages in his custody executed by marital law. These included Moyler and Tibbot Reagh Bourke, first cousins of Tibbot-ne-Long and 'the worst Bourks then living,'[25] according to Bingham. Other Bourke hostages in the keeping of the sheriff, John Browne, were also summarily executed, including Ulick, son of William, nicknamed the 'Blind Abbot'. All were accused, like Granuaile, of plotting to 'to draw in Scotts', the evidence for this being based mainly on hearsay and on dubious letters which were claimed to have been written by them from prison. But the importation of Scottish mercenaries was deemed a treasonable offence and Granuaile's life hung by a thread. Her reputation as a 'drawer in of Scots' was well established and Bingham now also wrote of her as the 'nurse to all rebellions in the province for forty years'.[27] But she was surprisingly set at liberty, as she later related, 'upon the hostage and pledge',[28] of her son-in-law, the Devil's Hook, who until this time had not openly joined in the rebellion. However, once he had secured Granuaile's freedom, he immediately joined his relations.

On her release, Granuaile lost little time in manning her fleet of galleys and heading north to Ulster, to ferry in the gallowglass. She was later to excuse her actions by maintaining that when the Devil's Hook went into rebellion 'fear compelled her to fly by sea into Ulster'[29] – an unlikely excuse, but politic and necessary under the circumstances in which she made it in 1593. En route to Ulster, she encountered a severe storm and her galleys were damaged. While they were been repaired, she took the opportunity to visit O'Neill and O'Donnell, the two most powerful chieftains in Ulster. She remained with them for three months. While the two clans were traditionally bitter enemies, under the then chieftain, Hugh Dubh O'Donnell, and the English-educated Hugh, Earl of Tyrone, the present *tanaiste* to the overall chieftaincy, old animosities had been laid aside. Both chieftains were beginning to realise that what was been visited on Connaught by Bingham and the English could soon extend to Ulster. Hugh O'Neill's second wife was O'Donnell's daughter. O'Donnell, who was married to the formidable Finola, the Ineen Dubh, daughter of James MacDónald, Lord of the Isles, cultivated close links with the royal court of Scotland.

There son, Red Hugh, one of the famous leaders of the later Ulster confederacy against the English, was then a youth, who after a few short months after Granuaile's visit to his father, like her would be a prisoner in Dublin Castle.

What matters Granuaile discussed with O'Neill and O'Donnell during her stay in Ulster in 1587 have not been documented. In Ulster, as in the rest of Ireland, rumours of a Spanish invasion of England were rife. Merchants and seamen carried stories of the mustering of ships, troops and arms in Spanish ports for an unprecedented attack on England. The Spanish king, Philip 11 was determined to embark on his crusade against Elizabeth, recently excumunicated by the Pope 'to visit the censure of God upon a middle-aged female',[30] and free England from heresy. The religious aspirations of the king's armada would have cut little ice with the Gaelic chieftains, but the political fall-out for themselves vis-á-vis the English was a different matter. The Ulster chieftains heard from Granuaile a first-hand account of Bingham's rule in Connaught and of his attempts to curb the power of the Gaelic chieftains there. With the intuition that was their hallmark, O'Neill and O'Donnell realised that the experiences of Munster and Connaught would inevitably be visited on them in Ulster unless English expansionism in Ireland could be reversed. But that would take some years yet to organise..

In Mayo Bingham executed by martial law the main contender for the MacWilliamship by Brehon law, the aged Edmund Bourke of Castlebar. In late September he defeated the huge force of Scots mercenaries who, with Granuaile's galleys out of commission, had made their own way by land into Mayo. On the banks of the Moy, Bingham routed them with great slaughter; 1,400 were accounted as having been killed of drowned. The rebellion subsequently collapsed and the Bourkes sued for peace. In May 1587, Elizabeth I ordered Bingham for service in Flanders. Seizing her chance, Granuaile set out for Dublin determined to take advantage of Bingham's absence. She was aware of the antagonism, now public knowledge, that existed between him and the Sir John Perrot, who had become Lord Deputy. Despite the evidence stacked against her, she wagered that so deep ran the antagonism between Perrot and Bingham, that any enemy of Bingham, no matter what treasonable offences she may have committed, was more than likely to receive a hearing from Perrot. And she wagered correctly. In Dublin, according to her testimony, she received 'her Majesty's pardon by Sir John Perrot'.[31] The pardon, preserved in the Elizabethan Fiants, also granted pardon for past offences against the crown to Granuaile's sons, Murrough O'Flaherty, Tibbot-ne-Long and to 'Margaret O'Flahertie daughter of Grany'.[32] The slate against Granuaile and her family was wiped clean. Granuaile's shrewdness had paid dividends, in the short term at least. She later claimed that on her return from Dublin, she lived 'in Connaught a farmer's life…and did give over her former trade of maintenance by sea and land.'[33] In reality, with Bingham out of the picture, she acquired additional galleys and resumed her seafaring enterprises with renewed vigour.

# CHAPTER SEVEN

# 'A Notable Traitoress'

On the evening of 29 July 1588 the long-threatened Spanish Armada was sighted off the Lizard. From beacon to beacon the news was relayed across England that King Philip of Spain's' meticulously planned crusade against his 'heretic' sister-in-law had become a reality. The 'invincible' armada of 134 ships and over 30,000 men, commanded by the flower of Spanish aristocracy, moved slowly and menacingly in a crescent formation along England's southern coast. After a series of naval skirmishes with the faster and more skilfully captained English fleet, the Armada ships became scattered. Fireships sent by the English among the great carracks, galleons and galleases wreaked further havoc. Then the elements took a hand. The wind shifted and the Spanish ships were driven up the Channel towards the North Sea pursued by the English fleet. On 21 August, the Armada set course to return to Spain, only to be buffeted by fierce storms and heavy seas, which drove the fleet towards the north and west costs of Ireland, where rocky headlands and awesome cliffs took a heavy toll of ships and men. In all, some twenty-six Armada ships were eventually wrecked on the Irish coast.

Fearing that the Spanish might land on the west coast of

Ireland and make common cause with the chieftains there, Sir Richard Bingham was hurriedly returned as Governor of Connaught. His adversary, Sir John Perrot, was recalled, and Sir William FitzWilliam replaced him as lord deputy. As the Armada ships were driven onto the Irish coast, and messengers and spies brought exaggerated tidings of great armies of Spanish soldiers holed up in coastal castles and towers, the English administration in Dublin, understrength and inadequately armed to repel such forces, panicked. FitzWilliam proclaimed it a crime punishable by death to harbour or aid Spanish castaways. Coupled with this, the Spanish ships were rumoured to contain untold treasure, the salvage of which was an added attraction for both English and Irish. Consequently, the Spanish survivors who managed to effect a landing on Irish soil, in the main, received a less than hospitable reception.

It was estimated that five ships were wrecked on Mayo's jagged coastline and that many of the survivors were summarily killed by treasure-seeking tribesmen. Given the remoteness and inaccessibility of the region, the inaccuracies – both deliberate and inadvertent – of English accounts, and the distinct lack of information from an Irish perspective, it is virtually impossible to assess the true story behind many of these wrecks. The single most controversial incident occurred on Clare Island, where, around 22 September, a huge ship, the square-rigged, cumbersome, converted merchantman, *El Gran Grin*, of some 1,160 tons, carrying 329 men and 28 guns when she sailed for England, was driven helplessly before the wind towards Clew Bay. With no space to manoeuvre she drifted onto Clare Island towards the cliffs on the southwest side, and was presumed to have been wrecked. English accounts record that her commander, Don Pedro de Mendoza, and about one hundred of the crew scrambled to safety but were eventually killed on the orders of Dubhdara Rua O'Malley. The remainder of the crew were drowned.

The facts regarding the wreck and supposed massacre are scanty. That *El Gran Grin* was driven towards the island is most likely true. That she was wrecked there and that her commander and crew were killed by the islanders is less certain. There is no deep-rooted tradition on the island of such a massacre having taking place. The O'Malleys, in particular, had been well used to piloting and trading with the Spanish for generations. Only the English accounts testify to the massacre, and these must be viewed in the context in which they were written.

On the other hand, the presence of some one hundred foreigners on Clare Island would undoubtedly have put the islanders under extreme pressure. Plunder and wrecking were part and parcel of seafaring life everywhere, and the O'Malleys were no exception to this custom. The foreigners more than likely outnumbered the islanders and, despite their plight, posed an imminent threat. To find food and shelter for so many would have put an immense strain on the island's slender resources. There is a mention in the English state papers that O'Malley had imprisoned the Spanish castaways initially, but that they had broken out and may well have attempted to fight their way off the island, commandeering the islanders' boats, on which their livelihoods depended. Three of the officers accredited to *El Gran Grin* were later identified as prisoners of Bingham in Galway. Whether O'Malley handed them over to the English or whether they were captured by the English bands, who constantly scoured the coastline for survivors, is uncertain. At this time the O'Malleys were one of the clans least likely to have co-operated freely with the English administration, particularly with Sir Richard Bingham. One way or another, whether the Spaniards were massacred by the O'Malleys, as the English reports claim, or were secretly taken off the island by them, either to a safe haven such as Scotland or reunited with the crews of other Armada vessels, the truth must rest beneath the fathoms with the many other secrets of the Armada wrecks.

A further complication to the theory of the Clare Island wreck is that it may have been mistaken for a ship that went aground at Fynglass (possibly present-day Toorglass) on the Corraun peninsula, a few miles from Granuaile's castle of Carraigahowley. Some accounts maintain that this was the 834-ton *San Nicholas Prodaneli*, while others claim that it was in fact *El Gran Grin*, which had been driven past Clare Island onto the mainland at Toorglass. The lands on which she was wrecked were claimed by the Earl of Ormond, 'Black' Tom Butler, as part of the original Anglo-Norman Butler estate. Black Tom was not slow to send messengers to Mayo with orders to make an inventory and lay claim to the ship's treasures, most of which by then had been picked clean by the local O'Malley and Bourke clansmen.

Among the reports concerning both wrecks in Clew Bay there is no mention of Granuaile. Whether she was absent on some business of her own or was too closely watched by Bingham's officers to intervene, is open to speculation. The lure of treasure and plunder was a way of life for her and there is no reason to assume that Spanish cargo would have been immune from her attention. Her attitude to the Spanish survivors was another matter. Her family's connections with Spain were long-established and her understanding of the Armada's ambitions may have been clearer to someone who had recently stayed with O'Neill, one of the few Gaelic chieftains who assisted the Spanish castaways. But, in any event, there was little she could have done to hide or protect the survivors, even if she had so desired.

Derided by FitzWilliam in Dublin for being ineffective in his pursuit of the Spanish survivors, Bingham directed his attention to the Connaught coastline. He ordered his deputy marshal, Robert Fowle, to seek out, dislodge and kill the unfortunate survivors. With her record by now well established, Granuaile's activities were closely monitored. That she assisted the Spanish survivors who came her way cannot be ruled out, especially since Bingham later testified that her son-in-law, the Devil's Hook from nearby Corraun, and his son, as well as the Bourkes of Erris and Sir Murrough-ne-Doe O'Flaherty in Iar-Chonnacht, all sheltered the Spanish who, he claimed, 'had an intention to remayne in the county of Mayo and that the inhabitants of the same were agreed to join with them…'[1]

Technically any chieftain found harbouring the Spanish was deemed by the English to in be in rebellion, and his lands forfeited to the crown.

It was a combination of the retention of the Spanish Armada survivors and the bad blood that existed between John Browne, the sheriff of Mayo, and the Bourkes of Corraun and Erris that sparked off the final Bourke rebellion in 1589. A controversial commission was issued to John Browne, by Bingham empowering him to enter the territory of the Burrishoole and Erris Bourkes:

> to prosecute and followe all and every of the said traytors…yt shall be lawful for you and yr, said companies to praie, burne and spolie…(giving them notice of the daunger thereof beforehand…[2]

The commission bore only Bingham's signature, instead of the two commissioners' signatures legally required. On

7 February 1589 the sheriff arrived at Granuaile's castle of Carraigahowley with an army of some 250 men. There he was met by the Devil's Hook's son, Richard Bourke, Granuaile's grandson, who objected to the sheriff's proposed entry through his territory. In the official correspondence relating to the incident, there is no mention of Granuaile, but in view of her previous attitude to English intruders on her property, it is certain that she would have found English presence at her castle as disagreeable as it had been before. Disregarding Richard Bourke's objection, Browne persisted and followed the main body of his army into Bourke territory. There he was attacked by the Devil's Hook's family and he together with his escort of some twenty-five soldiers were killed.

The Browne incident was a signal for the commencement of the most widespread rebellion in Connaught against the administration of Sir Richard Bingham. The Bourkes of Burrishoole, Corraun and Erris were joined by the Bourkes of Tirawley, the O'Malley's, Clandonnells and Clangibbons. Sir Murrough-ne-Doe O'Flaherty (despite the fact that his son was a hostage with Bingham and was subsequently executed) crossed Lough Corrib with an army of five hundred and joined the Bourkes. Granuaile, as Bingham reported, 'byrned and spoyled the isles of Aran',[3] which recently had been granted to an Englishman, Sir Thomas LeStrange. Her son, Tibbot-ne-Long, and his half-brother, Edmund, were named by Bingham as being among the rebel leaders. Mayo was in turmoil. The Bourkes raided Kilmaine and Clanmorris, taking substantial booty, and plundered right up to the very walls of Galway city.

Alarmed by the strength and extent of the rebellion, Lord Deputy FitzWilliam ordered Bingham to desist from any further action against the Bourkes, and a tentative truce was arranged. Negotiations with the English took place on the outskirts of Galway at Newcastle, the Bourke leaders having refused to come into Galway city. The contentious issue of the MacWilliamship title reared its head once again. The Bourkes demanded that Richard-an-Iarainn's brother, William Bourke, the Blind Abbot, *tánaiste* by Gaelic custom, should be restored to the title, and that Richard Bingham should be removed as governor of Connaught. Many in the English administration, including FitzWilliam, were in agreement with the second of their demands, which simply mirrored the conspiracy then afoot among Bingham's colleagues in the Irish service to have him removed from office.

Queen Elizabeth wrote of her disquiet at the rebellion in Connaught and urged FitzWilliam to adopt a conciliatory attitude to the Bourkes. FitzWilliam set out for Connaught, ordering Bingham to remain at Athlone. The appeasement policy proposed by the queen was beyond Bingham's comprehension. Angrily he wrote to a colleague at the English court:

> Truly I have not heard of the like between a prince and her subjects and much less with a race of such beggerly wretches as these... This dalliance with these rebels makes them most insolent and without the sword... it is impossible to govern the Irish people...[4]

On 12 June FitzWilliam met representatives of the Bourkes in St Nicholas' Church in Galway, where they presented him with a book of complaints against Bingham and his relations in the Connaught service. Granuaile was undoubtedly present as much of which Bingham stood accused of concerned his actions against her and her family. A similar book was also presented by the chieftains of Sligo against George Bingham, the governor's brother. Many charges were laid against Bingham, including breaches of the Composition, quartering of English soldiers on the people, and encroachments by officials in his administration on the lands and livings of the chieftains. Specific charges of murder, cruelty and torture were cited against him, including the murder of Granuaile's eldest son, Owen O'Flaherty, and her Bourke nephews; the hanging of the elderly chieftain, Edmund Bourke of Castlebar; and the execution of the young Bourke hostages, including Ulick, son of the Blind Abbot. The Bourkes made a token submission to the lord deputy, appropriately contrite in tone, and even promised that they would 'forthwith deliver to the lord deputy such Spaniards, Portugalls and other foreigners of the Spanish fleet as are now amongst them.'[5]

The submission was no more than a ploy to buy time. The Bourkes were careful not to hand over the customary hostages as a pledge to the agreement. On the other hand, they had prevailed on the lord deputy to curb English incursions on their lands and most significantly to remove Bingham from Connaught. The Bourkes knew that they held the advantage, with Mayo, part of Roscommon, Iar-Chonnacht, Sligo and Galway under their control. Granuaile, accompanied by one of her sons, went to Scotland to hire mercenaries. Their arrival back in Mayo in early September was reported to Bingham, who advised Burghley and the Privy Council that '7 gallies to be arryved in Erris with Scottes...having for their guyde and conductor one of Grany O'Malleys sons'.[6] However, Bingham's claim was refuted by no less a personage than the lord deputy who told Burghley, 'that she [Granuaile] shold be gon over into Scotland to drawe over Scotts into these parts...nothing could be untrulie written or reported...'[7]

and added, 'this man Bingham is shameless'. The result of the Bourke successes was the inauguration in October at Rousakeera of the Blind Abbot as the MacWilliam. The Bourkes and their confederates then recaptured Lough Mask Castle, part of the traditional seigniory of the MacWilliamship, and plundered the country from the Neale to Shrule.

As the rebellion steadily grew, Elizabeth's patience became exhausted and she ordered FitzWilliam to determine once and for all whether Bingham was guilty of the charges brought against him. After a trial in Dublin he was acquitted, and in spring 1590 he was free to return to his post in Connaught to bring the rebellion to an end. He immediately set about doing that in the only way he knew – by the sword. Aided by the earls of Clanrickard and Thomond, with an army of over one thousand, Bingham marched into Mayo and took Castlebar. From there he set out through the mountain pass of Barnagee and into Tirawley. Marching through the mountain fastness and boglands, he was shadowed by the Blind Abbot and Edmund Bourke with a small force of horsemen. The Bourkes launched a sudden attack, and in the ensuring skirmish the Blind Abbot's foot was cut off from the ankle. The Bourkes withdrew and ferried their injured leader across to a small island in Lough Conn. The Blind Abbot's foot had to be amputated, thereby ending his reign as The MacWilliam, his disability making him unfit to hold the title.

Bingham pressed home the advantage and marched through Tirawley and into Erris, relentlessly killing and plundering as he went. The people fled before him and hid themselves and their belongings in the mountain recesses. Bingham's army looted whatever they left behind and swept the land clean of livestock. By the time he left Erris, Bingham had amassed a herd of over two thousand cattle, taken from the people. Arriving in Burrishoole, he found that most of the inhabitants had fled before him for safety into the islands in Clew Bay. For lack of boats, he was unable to pursue them, but he took retribution, as he recorded, of '100 cows and slew all the churls, women and children.'[8] The rebellion began to crumble. The Clandonnells, the standing army of the Bourkes, were first to submit, and they were followed by the leaders of the Bourkes and their allies, with the exception of the sept of Ulick Bourke, led by Granuaile's stepson, Edmund, and her son, Tibbot-ne-Long, who in June 1591 ambushed John Bingham near Cloonagashal in Mayo.

Granuaile aided her son and stepson, and her territory around Carraigahowley bore the brunt of Bingham's retribution. While she was at sea her land was devastated, picked clean by Bingham's hordes. The sea was now her sole refuge. With her galleys she swooped again on the Aran Islands where, as Bingham later testified against her, she 'committed some spoile…to the value of 20 mark.'[9]

Bingham gave her no respite. When news was brought to her that her second son, Murrough-ne-Maor O'Flaherty, had submitted and was now an ally of her arch enemy, Bingham, her fury knew no bounds. She vowed to teach him a lesson. Like his peers, Murrough-ne-Maor was concerned only with his personal vendetta against a neighbour, Sir Murrough-ne-Doe O'Flaherty and his son who had previously attacked his ancestral lands. Operating a divide and rule policy, Bingham offered to assist him against them, in return for Murrough's allegiance. But Grace was having none of it. Her attack on her son was later communicated by Bingham to Queen Elizabeth's senior statesman, William Cecil, Lord Burghley in an attempt to discredit her further at court.

> His (Murrough's) aforesaid mother Grany (being out of
> charety with her sonne for serving her Matie.) manned
> out her Navy of Galleys  and landed in Ballinehencie
> where he dwelleth, burned his towen and spoiled his
> people of their cattayle and goods and murdered 3 or 4
> of his men which offered to make resistence...[10]

Bingham cites this incident to Burghley, hoping 'to gyve
your Honour Knowledge of her naughty disposicion towards
the state.'[11] Little is heard of Murrough-ne-Maor in the war
against Bingham after Granuaile's action against him. That
Granuaile would take arms against her own son is testimony
to her grim determination in pursuit of her aims, allowing
neither maternal instinct nor emotional ties to get in the way.
It also demonstrates a lack of favouritism on her part, in that
she was prepared to admonish kith and kin when she felt it
necessary.

In June 1591 a force of seven hundred Scottish mercenaries
arrived in Erris seeking employment from the Bourkes in the
war against Bingham. In an attempt to secure payment for their
futile journey, they ravaged north Mayo which had barely
recovered from the excesses of Bingham's army. In the mêlée
that followed, some of Granuaile's Bourke and O'Malley
relations were killed, including two of the Blind Abbot's sons.
Granuaile hurried northwards to help, but by the time she
arrived in Erris the Scots had fled by sea back to Scotland.
Undaunted, Granuaile gave chase in her galleys, as Bingham
reported to the Privy Council, hoping, as he stated sardonically,
'that all or the moste part will take their journy towardes heaven
and the province ridd of manie badd and ill disposed persons.'[12]
Bingham's hope was not fulfilled because Granuaile survived
the journey and continued to be a thorn in his side. Her actions
demonstrate the lengths to which she was prepared to go to

avenge a wrong committed against her extended family, and how she in turn was looked to as their legitimate protector and avenger – a privilege and a duty formerly deemed the sole preserve of the elected male chieftain.

With the removal of the Blind Abbot as a contender for leadership of the Mayo Bourkes, and the death during 1591 of most of the senior aspirants, Granuaile's stepson, Edmund, and her son, Tibbot-ne-Long, emerged as the principal leaders in the Bourke hierarchy. Together with Granuaile, they were the two remaining chieftains who by spring 1592 had not submitted to Bingham. In the struggle between the English and Gaelic worlds in Mayo, no likely victor had as yet emerged. Under Bingham, English control had undoubtedly advanced. Yet, as the various Bourke rebellions had demonstrated, when confronted by a Gaelic alliance, English power was quite fragile. However, despite their victories over the English, the Bourkes and their allies suffered from the prevailing Gaelic malaise – Gaelic leaders in Mayo and elsewhere, including Granuaile and her sons, fought merely their own corner. Their only spur was, as it had been for their ancestors, that of survival in the political as well as the physical sense. They were products of their time and of a society which still nurtured the outmoded Celtic tradition of independent and fragmented tribalism, which seemed incapable of producing a single centralised authority. Gaelic Ireland had fallen behind the rest of Europe. As one historian has written:

> such a life had been an anachronism in the medieval system and there was no place for it in Renaissance Europe...the fundamental divergence between the Celtic conception of a ruler and the new conception of the state. [13]

This tribalism, when coupled with the divide and conquer strategy about to be introduced on a wider scale by the English in Mayo to accelerate the conquest there, and which would see Bourke turn on Bourke, clan on clan, would ensure the ultimate downfall of the Gaelic system, unless the Gaelic powers could combine and present a united front against the English.

The first inkling of Mayo being drawn into a wider net of opposition to the English crown occurred in the spring of 1592. Tibbot-ne-Long was approached by bishops Hely and O'Boyle to raise a rebellion in Mayo in tandem with Red Hugh O'Donnell, the young chieftain of Tirconail, lately escaped from captivity in Dublin Castle. Spanish aid was promised, and the prospect of re-establishing the MacWilliamship was held out as an additional incentive. Tibbot-ne-Long reacted cautiously. The concept of waging battle at the behest and in the cause of an outsider, particularly an O'Donnell of Tirconail, was an unfamiliar one. Moreover, since the last rebellion, Bingham had Mayo firmly under control and had established a garrison at Castlebar, cutting off the western Bourkes from their traditional allies in the north of the county. However, on the appeal of the Clandonnells to rescue one of their leaders imprisoned by Bingham at Cloonagashal, Tibbot-ne-Long initiated a rising in Mayo and attacked Cloonagashal where Bingham was holding sessions. The attack was beaten back by the garrison. Tibbot-ne-Long held out until he heard that O'Donnell himself had submitted and that the Spanish aid had not materialised.

Tibbot-ne-Long's actions brought the full wrath of Bingham once more down on Burrishoole, with disastrous consequences for Granuaile, who was still operating from nearby Carraigahowley Castle. Since Bingham's devastation of her territory, during the late rebellion, the sea had again become her sole source of survival and she was desperately trying to regroup and replenish what Bingham had destroyed. Now in retaliation for her son's attack on Cloonagashal, Bingham entered her territory and again stripped it bare of cattle and produce. But this time he also penetrated Granuaile's sea domain, something he had failed to do previously. He wrote to the Privy Council:

> At Burrishoole we met our shipping and so continued there two nights altogether. The shipping has done great service for the same had cleared all their islands. [14]

With English warships in Clew Bay, the secrets that had maintained Granuaile's seapower for so long were revealed. The network of harbours, islands, channels and fortresses that had hidden her activities along the west coast and given her the freedom of movement her trade by sea required, were now exposed. There was nowhere she could hide and nowhere to where the ships could run before the wind, laden with booty, and be safe from pursuit. Bingham's invasion of her sea domain and his subsequent impounding of most of her fleet was a major reversal of fortune and one from which she was never to recover fully.

There is an intriguing entry in the state papers for later in 1599, referring to the galleys then in the possession of Granuaile and Tibbot-ne-Long, which states that they had been forcibly taken by them from 'an Englishman of Sir Richard Bingham's, who was there killed.'[15] Perhaps after Bingham's departure from Connaught in 1595 Granuaile struck back, by seizing the English galleys in lieu of those of hers impounded by Bingham.

For Tibbot-ne-Long further resistance was futile. In September 1592 he submitted to Bingham at Aghagower:

'Tibbott Burke Mac Richard-an-Iarainn came into us and agreed into all things for the Burkes, O'Malleys and Clangibbons to be received into her Majesty's mercy and protection laying in his foster-father Edmund MacTibbot and one Tibbot Mac Gibbon to remain as pledges...'[16] The terms of surrender were severe. Bingham set out to reduce the influence of chieftains like Tibbot-ne-Long by stripping them of the foundation on which their power existed – their client chieftains. Henceforth, a chieftain could represent his own sept only . Tibbot-ne-long was required to pay a proportion of the cost of the army Bingham had brought into Mayo to quell the rebellion, and to make restitution for the spoils committed. He was also fined a certain number of cattle. Well might Bingham write after this that Tibbot-ne-Long and his step-brother Edmund were 'men of no possessions or to have of any goods so much as half a dozen cows apiece.'[17]

An uneasy peace descended on Mayo, devastated by the long series of wars and disorder which had reduced it to a wilderness. Politically the inadequacies of the age-old Gaelic system had been cruelly exposed and as cruelly dismantled by the relentless pressure of Richard Bingham's harsh régime. More than most, Granuaile had been a victim of Bingham's oppression. Now in her sixties, an astonishing age in the sixteenth century, especially given the perilous career she had chosen, she saw the Gaelic world of her ancestors crumble before Bingham's onslaught. The unique role that she had carved out for herself had been diminished and she was reduced to the status of dependent widowhood. While it could be said that time rather than any one individual had finally caught up Granuaile and with the antiquated Gaelic world that had bred and bore her, she knew with certainty that one man alone had been instrumental in reducing her both in power and in wealth. Her eldest son murdered, her second son under the heel of her enemy, her ships, cattle and horse herds confiscated, her territory destroyed and, most of all, her freedom of movement, especially by sea, restricted – all had as their source her arch-enemy, Sir Richard Bingham. For another of similar age, sex and circumstances, it would have been understandable to have surrendered to such seemingly insurmountable difficulties, to have laid down the sword and bowed to the inevitable. But not for someone who had fought for survival for over forty years, who had fearlessly sailed the wild western coastline, who had endured imprisonment and deprivation, who had fought with sword in hand by land and sea, who had negotiated with every major figure in the English administration in Connaught for thirty years and, as a later poet wrote of her, one who had

> …dared the tempest in its midnight wrath
> And through opposing billows cleft her fearless path.[18]

it was simply not in her character, even at this late stage of her life, to capitulate. And in the spring of 1593 in her stark fortress of Carraigahowley, Granuaile was already plotting her next move.

# CHAPTER EIGHT

# The Meeting of the Two Queens

Many factors prompted Granuaile to put her case directly before Queen Elizabeth I. Equally many reasons could have inhibited her from so doing. The reasons for her decision are evident in her correspondence to the Queen and to the Queen's privy councillors, especially to her Treasurer, Lord Burghley. The factors that might have prohibited her stem more from a misconception of the political context pertaining to sixteenth century Gaelic Ireland and the motivations that governed the political actions of the majority of Gaelic leaders there. Perhaps this single episode in Granuaile's chequered life contributed most to her exclusion from Irish historical records. Later generations of historians, intent on eulogising previous generations of Irish heroes, could find no place for one who it seemed had 'bended the knee' to perfidious Albion. On the other hand, folklore, legend and poetry conversely sought to place a patriotic gloss on Granuaile's meeting with the Queen of England by fashioning it into a meeting of two queens of equal standing, with the Irish queen getting the upperhand of her rival. Somewhere in between lies the reality.

Political conditions obtaining in Ireland at the time of Granuaile's journey to the English court were, to say the least convoluted. The native system was being steadily eroded by a power that in Connaught had, as it had a decade earlier in the Munster of Granuaile's old adversary the Earl of Desmond, fallen foul of the power and tactics of a determined usurper. The society that supported individual chieftains like Granuaile was slowly but surely dying. Its stagnation in a heroic time warp, its sheer inflexibility and obstinacy to become part of a world that had swept away the final vestiges of medievalism elsewhere, had become the trap within which it must surely perish, taking with it those chieftains who continued to champion its cause. Gaelic resistance was piecemeal, undisciplined and lacked a coherent and unifying policy. Most importantly it lacked a centralising authority, a figurehead which in England was embodied in the person of Elizabeth Tudor. The Gaelic code, with its emphasis on the individual rather than on the commonweal, seemed incapable of producing such a leader. Gaelic chieftains were still more apt to fight one another than to consolidate against the English. The result of Mayo's fragmented resistance to English power, to which Granuaile had contibuted, lay in ruins. The leadership hierarchy in Mayo, through death and execution, was decimated. The land lay waste and bare. English garrisons established in the forfeited castles of the chieftains monitored every movement. Granuaile had suffered more than most: death of kith and kin, imprisonment, impoverishment, confiscations and above all the seizure of her ships. At sixty three years of age without any means of support, her future looked bleak.

Granuaile was a product of the Gaelic world of her birth and rearing. Her quarrel was not with the state of England or its queen. but with the individual representatives of England with whom she had come into conflict. She had experienced at first-hand the traits and tactics used by conqueror and coloniser since the beginning of time: the promises and pacts, made and broken, then the ambiguity and deception, finally the ruthless subjugation as the incomprehension and incompatibility between the Gaelic and English worlds exploded into bloody confrontation. When the representatives of the English world, like Sidney and Perrot, appeared to deal with her in a way that did not unduly dilute her power and freedom, then she, like most of her fellow chieftains, was prepared to deal, even to make token submissions. The earlier breed of Elizabethan officials like Sidney were content, for the most part, to be facilitators of such nominal submissions in order to preserve the peace and to avoid, on their queen's orders, expensive warfare. But international politics and changing religious and social attitudes in England eventually impacted on Ireland to give a more urgent and ruthless edge to its conquest.

It was the age of exploration and discovery of new lands to conquer, of fortunes to be made. For many Englishmen, Ireland offered a less distant target to fulfil such ambitions than the far-off Americas. After the death of the Earl of Desmond and the collapse of the Desmond rebellion in 1583, the once repugnant Irish service became more attractive, especially when Desmond's 500,000 acres, innumerable castles, woodlands, fisheries and limitless rights and tributes in Munster were parcelled out among the avaricious victors. The spoils attracted a new breed of English adventurer. Younger sons of landed gentry, lawyers and entrepreners, who saw in Ireland's disordered political state, her rich pasturelands and virgin forests, the way to personal fortunes.

In tandem with exploration and discovery comes exploitation. The natives over whom these English adventurers hoped to rule had to be presented as rebels, as a race unfit to govern themselves, unworthy to own such prime lands and properties, a race inferior in every way. If they could be provoked to rebel, like Desmond, then by English law their lands and properties were automatically forfeited and could be picked up at a nominal cost. The bigoted strain of the new, puritanical, religious fervour that was sweeping England and that, to her unease and personal dislike, had infiltrated Elizabeth's administration, added another dimension to fuel incompatability and hatred between native and newcomer. For the first time religion had been introduced as a divisive issue in Ireland. Sir Richard Bingham, his family and many in his administration in Connaught epitomised many or all of these English traits and Granuaile had borne the brunt of their anatagonism, prejudice and cruelty.

It is against this background that Granuaile opened correspondence with the Queen of England in June 1593. Her motivation was primarily one of survival, to get Bingham off her back. There was no one in the Irish administration to whom she could turn. Bingham had successfully crushed the Bourke rebellion and his success had, for the present, silenced his critics in the Irish council. It is obvious that Granuaile was aware of how the English administration operated and was sufficiently aware of the political process to know that a direct approach to the Queen was both feasible and was now her only recourse. She was also sufficiently confident in her ability to navigate her way through the labyrinthine channels of Tudor officialdom. How her first petition to the Queen, written for her while she was still in Ireland, was delivered to the court is unclear. One of her later petitions was endorsed by the powerful Earl of Ormond, Black Tom, then a favourite of Elizabeth.

Through the grant made to his ancestors in the twelfth century, he had recently revived a claim to part of the barony of Burrishoole where Granuaile lived.

With characteristic cunning, diplomacy and a sophisticated ability to negotiate, knowing that Bingham has already fed the Queen damning evidence of her long career as a pirate and rebel, Granuaile firstly establishes her version of events. In the opening lines of her petition she informed Elizabeth:

> ...of the continnual discord stirrs and dissention that hertofore long tyme remained among the Irishrye especialy in west Conaght by the sea side everie cheeftaine for his safeguard and maintenance and for the defence of his people, followers and countrye took armes by strong hand to make head against his neybours which in like manner constrayned your highness fond subject to take armes and by force to maintaine her selfe and her people by sea and
> land the space of fortye years past....[1]

Then in almost chatty vein she tells of her two marriages, her sons and then her present situation as a widow. She claims that the Gaelic system as it operated in Connaught never yielded 'thirds' to the widows of chieftains who, because of the disordered state of their territories and their constant warring, on their deaths had little to leave in any event. She also takes the English-imposed Composition of Connaught to task for neglecting to make provision for the widows of chieftains. She asks:

> ...in tender consideracion whereof and in regard of her great age... to grant her some reasonable maintenance for the little tyme she hath to lyve...[2]

She offers the Queen 'a surrender at her hands' of the lands of her two sons and also the lands of her two remaining Bourke nephews. Then seizing the opportunity to achieve her main objective, to return to the sea and circumvent Bingham's embargo, she boldly asks the Queen to

> ...grant unto your said subject under your most gracious hand of signet free libertye during her lyve to envade with sword and fire all your highness enemies wheresoever they are or shall be... (and the crunch clause) without any interuption of any person or persons whatsoever...

It was an ingenious stroke to return to her old ways but this time with the Queen's personal approval, thereby making herself untouchable by Bingham and his ilk.

While her petition made its way by sea to London, an incident occurred which lent it new urgency. Ulster was secretly preparing for war, urged on by the twin fears of the extension of English power into the last bastion of Gaelic-controlled territory and a renewed hope of Spanish assistance. The English-educated Earl of Tyrone, Hugh O'Neill, now chieftain of the great O'Neill clan, amidst great subterfuge and outward protestations of loyalty to the Queen, had secretly confederated with the young Tirconail chieftain, Red Hugh O'Donnell. Tyrone had seen first-hand what had happened in Munster where, as a loyal ally of the Crown, he had ridden with the English hordes as they lay the rich lands of the Earl of Desmond to waste and had seen the dead earl's patrimony parcelled out among the victors. Nearer home he had seen Bingham's subjugation of Connaught. Now the English were knocking on the doors of Ulster. Breifny had been burned and looted by Bingham's bands. The whole of Monaghan had been proclaimed, its chieftain MacMahon executed. Next in line to face the English onslaught was Maguire's country of Fermanagh. Still on the sidelines Tyrone waited and watched the build-up of Gaelic resentment against English excesses, fanned by a new wave of the Counter Reformation exhortations of Irish clerics returning from the Papal and Spanish courts, seeth and intensify.

Reduced in power and wealth by Bingham, any road to reverse the deprivation was welcome to Granuaile's son Tibbot-ne-Long. When in May 1593, Maguire finally broke out and burnt Ballymote, then under the control of Sir George Bingham, one of Maguire's men captured by Bingham was alleged to have implicated Tibbot-ne-Long in Tyrone's Ulster conspiracy, as Bingham reported:

> Tibbot Burke had even then written a lettre in Irishe to Brian oge O'Rourke to raise sturres in the Breny and to hold out but two monthes and he would undertak that the banished rebell the Devills Hoke and the rest should retourne to Mayo againe and with his help mak warres...[3]

Bingham promptly clapped Tibbot-ne-Long in prison in Athlone on a charge of treason. In the heightened political situation the air was thick with claim and counterclaim, subterfuge and intrigue. Tibbot's imprisonment by her avowed enemy galvanised Granuaile into action, to undertake the most hazardous voyage of her career. Haste was imperative if she was to save her son's life. Treason was punishable by death and she had every reason to believe that Bingham would not be slow to invoke the law against her son, or even worse, as she later explained to Queen Elizabeth.

> The poor youth of the countrey are so extreamly used as they are most comonly executed before they be justly tryed or ther cause only hearde...[4]

Coupled with the imprisonment of her son, her half-brother, Dónal-ne-Piopa O'Malley, who resided at the clan fortress of Cathair-na-mart, was also arrested by Bingham and charged with the murder of some soldiers. Very little was heard of this O'Malley during the late rebellions and, as his nickname suggests, he perhaps was either more given to playing the pipes or drinking wine, than making war.

Folklore and tradition maintain that Granuaile captained one of her own ships for the voyage to England and there is certainly no reason to doubt her capability in this regard. Folklore and tradition also state that she was accompanied by a troop of her hardy kerne and that barefoot, dressed in her Irish costume, the beautiful, young Irish 'queen' cut an outlandish figure in the court of Queen Elizabeth, then the epitome of style. It is said that it was the meeting of two queens of equal standing and when the two women were introduced, Elizabeth held out her hand, but Granuaile being taller, the English queen was forced to raise her hand to the Irish queen. It was perceived that during the course of their meeting Granuaile required a handkerchief and Elizabeth lent her a fine cambric one, edged with lace. Upon using it, Granuaile threw it into the nearby fire bringing the surprised retort from Elizabeth that it was meant to be put in her pocket. Equally surprised, Granuaile told her that in her country they had a higher standard of cleanliness. When Elizabeth offered to confer the title of countess on Granuaile, she is said to have declined the offer on the basis that a title could not be conferred on one of equal status. When Elizabeth bemoaned the cares of royalty, looking around her sumptuous surroundings, Granuaile witheringly told her 'that the poor women of Mayo had greater cares and greater industry to their credit.'[5]

It is not surprising that the meeting of perhaps two of the

most flamboyant historical characters of the century would not give rise to such fanciful tales, particularly in Ireland, where the mainly oral tradition of storytelling over the centuries would have embellished details of the meeting. The factual evidence relating to the meeting rests solely on the correspondence of Granuaile, Lord Burghley, Sir Richard Bingham, Tibbot-ne-long, the Earl of Ormond and Queen Elizabeth. That Granuaile was at Court from June until September 1593 is certain and in the course of that time she was granted an audience with Elizabeth. The circumstances both leading up to the visit, the reasons for it and the outcome, though vastly different from the folklore and fiction, are just as fascinating.

Granuaile did not go alone on her journey to England. She was accompanied by at least three other people, who were expressely mentioned as having come to Court with her. One was her first husband's old adversary and first cousin, the elderly O'Flaherty chieftain, Sir Murrough-ne-Doe, who sought redress against a relation, a protege of Sir Richard Bingham, who had encroached on his property. Granuaile is also said by Bingham to 'have carryed over into England,'[6] the son of Ulick Bourke of Erris and her grand-nephew, the son of Tibbot Reagh Bourke who, according to an English official 'attended uppon Grany O'Maille at her late beyinge at Court.'[7] This implies that she sailed her own ship there and consequently would have been accompanied by more of her men, but who may not necessarily have appeared with her at court. Her age, although she was not averse to use it as bargaining ploy with Elizabeth and Burghley, did not mitigate against her from seafaring, as her exploits by sea, as late as 1597, prove. Consequently in 1593, physically she was still well capable of captaining her ship to England. The south coast of Ireland was familiar territory to her and well within the capabilities of one who was used to longer voyages in more treacherous waters. Her journey was, nonetheless, daunting. Few Gaelic chieftains with such a long-established record of rebellion and piracy would have dared put a foot on English soil, particularly in the prevailing political climate of intrigue with Sapin. Granuaile must have possessed great confidence in her powers of persuasion that her case would be heard, that she would attain an audience with the Queen and that she would not be hanged. Rumours abounded of another Spanish invasion and the seas around the southern coasts of Ireland and England were patrolled by English warships. The capture of an Irish ship, captained by a notorious pirate leader, would have been no mean prize for any privateer.

Nothing daunted she sailed her ship around the south coast, past the Old Head of Kinsale and into St George's Channel, past Land's End and, the Scilly Isles, through the straits of Dover and finally into the narrow estuary of the Thames, to anchor at one of the many landing places below London Bridge. There the Irish galley must have been dwarfed by the bulk and soaring mast-heads of international shipping in the port of London, then one of the busiest and wealthiest in the world. All along the bustling waterfront ships from Antwerp, Hamburg, Bordeaux, Venice and the Levant discharged cargos of wines, spices, silk, carpets, metalware, pottery, glassware, pitch, and timber and were loaded with English produce: tin, corn, coal and the lucrative woven cloth. Barges, lighters and the traditional river wherries, constantly ferried passengers and products up and down the teeming highway that was the Thames. Upriver towards the palaces of Whitehall and Westminster the new mansions of wealthy merchants and influential aristocrats rose imposingly above the waterside. Behind the facade of wealth and commerce lay the crowded, noisy streets of London, reverberating to the shrill cry of trader, shopkeeper and huckster and permeated by the stench of open sewer and rotting refuse. Through the narrow streets and laneways, bounded on either side by wooden-framed houses, shops and taverns, a constant mass of people jostled and pushed their way: tradesmen, porters, pickpockets, beggers, drovers, driving herds of sheep, cattle and pigs, vied for position with sword-swinging aristocrats spoiling for a fight and richly attired ladies, perfumed handkerchiefs held at the ready to stifle the stench as they flitted from goldsmith to haberdasher. All was noise and movement, a far cry from the pastoral setting of the west of Ireland.

Granuaile's impressions of this vast metropolis must remain in the realm of fiction and fancy. Like every visitor to London during the reign of Elizabeth, she was doubtless impressed by the city's vibrancy and wealth as much as she was repelled by the stench, filth and the overcrowding. As one who had spent her lifetime on the open invigorating seas and in the underpopulated Irish countryside, city life must have been an anathema. Her mission, however, was not to sightsee or trade with merchant or shopkeeper, but to barter with the Queen of England for her freedom and for the life of her son.

Elizabeth moved her court regularly from one palace to the next. During the summer months, when disease flourished in London, she progressed between her country palaces such as Richmond, Hampton Court, Nonsuch and especially Greenwich. In the summer of 1593, an outbreak of the plague had sent the court scurrying out of the city to the more salubrious air of the countryside. Tradition has always held that it was at Greenwich Palace on the banks of the

Thames that Granuaile finally met with Queen Elizabeth.

From the evidence to hand it is clear that from early July Granuaile was in England. Like the hundreds of petitioners who hung about the fringes of the Court intent on capturing the Queen's ear, Granuaile had to conform to the required protocol and wait her turn. Great formality attached to the court of Elizabeth and access to the Queen was difficult and restrictive. Other than the notorious meeting of Elizabeth and Shane O'Neill in 1562, few Irish chieftains were recorded as having been granted access to the Queen. Granuaile was not the only Irish petitioner at court that summer. She herself mentions the presence of her son's brother-in-law, Sir Donogh O'Connor Sligo, who had also come to seek redress against the Binghams. There too was, Eleanor Butler FitzGerald, the tragic widow of the 'rebel' Earl of Desmond, Granuaile's gaoler in 1577. Stripped of the vast wealth, lands and property enjoyed by her husband which, since his death in 1583, had been snapped up by such court personalities as Sir Walter Raleigh, the poet Edmund Spenser, Warham St Leger and Sir Christopher Hatton, the Countess of Desmond, had been forced to beg her bread on the streets of Dublin. Her son, the rightful heir, was a prisoner, shut away and forgotten in the grim dungeons of the Tower of London. Her story was a sobering example of the cruel and retributive obverse of the glittering coin of Elizabethan achievements, of which Granuaile had experienced her fill in Connaught.

The year 1593 was a time of great political unease in England. The prospect of another Spanish invasion loomed large as English privateers like Raleigh, Howard, Frobisher and Grenville, continued to attack the King of Spain's treasure ships returning from the New World. Across the Channel, Philip was attempting to gain a foothold on the western coast of France and Elizabeth strove to keep him out at all costs. The Queen's support of the Protestant French king, Henry of Navarre, against the French Catholic League, which was supported in turn by Philip, received a setback in July. Deciding that his alliance with England could no longer guarantee him immunity from Philip, Henry of Navarre decided to turn Catholic, declaring that *Paris vaut une messe* (Paris was worth a mass). His decision provoked great unease in the English court, which feared an alliance between France and Spain, leaving Protestant England and the Netherlands to stand alone against the Spanish threat. The Court circles throbbed with rumour and counter-rumour and with the toing and froing of diplomatic delegations, ambassadors, emissaries and spies.

Granuaile opened her campaign to gain access to the Queen firstly through Black Tom, the tenth Earl of Ormond, cousin and favourite of the Queen, who gave her an introduction to the Lord Treasurer, Lord Burghley, then the most powerful man in the Queen's service. Referred to by Elizabeth as 'her spirit', William Cecil had served his temperamental and autocratic royal mistresss loyally and long. Now in his seventy-third year, gout and old age had slowed him physically but mentally he was as vigilant in the Queen's interest as he had always been. Subterfuge, diplomacy, patronage, even murder, he employed during his long tenure, to ensure the mission for which life had ordained him – to serve his queen and fulfil the criteria she had demanded of him when she first became queen:

'that you will not be corrupted with any manner of gift; and you will be faithful to the State and, without respect of my private will, you will give me the counsel that you think best.'[8]

For the space of his long career, William Cecil had negotiated, outwitted and outmanouevered the best minds in Europe as he steered his sovereign through the traumatic years of her reign.

It was to this most able world statesman to whom Granuaile turned in her need and to whom she was later to refer to as her 'best frende since her cominge hyther.'[9] The Queen's secretary was not ignorant about Granuaile, in fact he knew more about her than she perhaps realised. From Sir Henry Sidney to Bingham, for the space of twenty years, he had read in the despatches of those employed in the Irish service about this woman leader from Connaught. He had written her name and doodled her pedigree and complex family connections in his own hand on various state documents which detailed her nefarious activities. But before he advanced her petition to the Queen, he determined to know more. To this effect, he forwarded her a list of 'eighteen articles of interrogatory to be answered by Grany ne Mally.'[10] (see appendices) The questions and the answers given by Granuaile are preserved in the Elizabethan state papers and bear observations in the margin written in Burghley's own hand. They provide not only an informative resumé of Granuaile's life, her family and relations, her observations and opinions on the social and political practices obtaining in her native Connaught during that period, but they are also testimony to the depth of her political accumen. She gives an account of her life, especially since the death of Richard-an-Iarainn, as well as her version of events leading up to her arrest by Bingham and her narrow escape from hanging at his hands. She speaks of the tragic death of her eldest son, Owen O'Flaherty, and throws suspicion on Bingham's brother for his murder. Her flight into Ulster to O'Neill, whom she is well aware is now under suspicion of collusion with Spain, she explains, was out of fear of reprisal by Bingham. She tells of her pardon received from Sir John Perrot in Dublin. Her replies are always guarded and she concentrates on aspects of her life least objectionable to the English. She adroitly neglects to mention her participation in the Bourke rebellions, her plundering exploits by land and sea, her collusion with O'Neill and O'Donnell, both suspect by the English of plotting with Spain, and her importation of Scottish mercenaries. Her replies show a cunning subtlety and are a match for Burghley's machiavellian mind.

While she awaited response to the articles, a letter came to court hotfoot from Sir Richard Bingham in Ireland who had only lately learned that

> ...there be 2 notable traitors gon over Sir Morrow ne doe and Grainy O'Maly both rebelle from their childhoode and continually in accion...for notwithstanding that they have many pardons there ys matter ynough of late found out against them to hang them by justice...[11]

Knowing full well that the two petitioners would have little positive to say on his behalf he sought to preempt their accusations.

> ...if they be drawen to make generall exclamations against me, I do not doubt but your honour will most honorably and indifferently consyder of it... [12]

Bingham's damning indictment did not adversely affect Granuaile's chances. Her replies to Burghley's questions seem to have been at one satisfactory and intriguing enough for the Queen to wish to see her. That Granuaile undoubtedly had support at Court is commented on by Bingham disgruntled, at 'having bin advertised from thence that some in Court hath comended her for doing her Matie good service...'[13] There was trouble brewing in Ulster and stories of the Earl of Tyrone's intrigue with Spain and of a confederacy forming between the Ulster chieftains sent shivers of unease down English backs lest Ireland would join with Spain and France in one grand alliance against Elizabeth. To pardon rather than to punish past offenders, to maintain an influential leader like Granuaile in some semblance of loyalty was, given the political atmosphere then prevailing, despite Bingham's objections, from Burghley's perspective, a far wiser course to follow.

Later in July, Granuaile finally received her summons to appear before the Queen. Elizabeth was at the apex of her power, the beloved Gloriana of her people, the 'Goddesse Heavenly Bright' of Edmund Spenser's *Faerie Queene*, Good Queen Bess, the saviour of England from the tyranical ambitions of Spain. For thirty-five years she had steered England safely through turbulent political waters, by a strategy of delay, procrastination, secrecy, compromise and prudence, and had proved her worth and her right to rule. While she may have had 'the body of a weak and feeble woman', she had shown that she possessed, as she told her troops at Tilbury in 1588, when the Armada was bearing down on England's shores, 'the heart and stomach of a king, and a king of England too.'[14] By sheer graft, personality and an inherited Tudor belief in her God-given right to rule, this bastard daughter of Henry VIII and Anne Boleyn, without a clear title to the throne, had won the respect and adoration of all England.

She could be coarse and bawdy, she spat and picked her teeth, was given to swearing, had a temper to match her red hair and boxed the ears of her ministers, who constantly despaired of her making up her mind. A brillant scholar and linguist, she had a cruel wit and a razor-sharp tongue. She bullied and cajoled her flamboyant, quarrelsome courtiers like children and demanded and received their dying devotion and symbolic love. In her sixtieth year, age had not spared even the deified figure of Elizabeth Tudor. Her eyes peered shortsightedly out of her sharp-featured face, her red hair had given way to a wig, her face was a mask of rice powder and rouge, her nose 'grew hooked as a harridan's,'[15] and her teeth were decayed and blackened. What age had ravaged, Elizabeth Tudor sought to conceal by the sheer opulence and radiance of her wardrobe and she strutted through her court dressed like some exotic bird.'

> The Queen's dresses were not distinguished by refinement of taste: it was rather at a magnificent display that she aimed and her predilection was for gowns richly embroidered and sewn with jewels, so that they were as encrusted with ornament as the buildings of the early English Renaissance.'[16]

This then was the vain, autocratic, supreme ruler with whom Granuaile sought to do business. The similarities between them were marked. They were around the same age. Both were women who had usurped what was perceived to be a man's role and of whom their respective laws had sought to deprive of power. By sheer determination, example and obstinacy they had both prevailed and won. Both were well used to ruling men, to having their orders obeyed, as the poet wrote of Granuaile

> She seemed well used to power, as one that hath
> Dominion over men of savage mood...[17]

Both displayed a certain magnetism, a charisma which kept their followers in thrall and loyal until the end of their lives.

Both sought to protect their 'country' and their power from the excesses of whatever enemy who sought to deprive them of it. For Elizabeth, the enemy was Spain: for Granuaile, the enemy was Elizabeth's military men in Connaught.

Age and the harsh environment in which she operated had undoubtedly left its imprint on Granuaile. Unlike Elizabeth, the furrows and wrinkles of age, salt spray and wind lay exposed for all to see on her face. It is unlikely that she could survive her long battle with the elements and her enemies over the space of forty years without some outward scar or blemish. Granuaile's dress, while doubtless of the finest available in her wardrobe, was hardly a match or indeed a threat to the opulance of the Queen.

In other respects blatant differences existed between them. Each represented a culture totally incompatible and incomprehensible one to the other and which were embarked on a collision course from which there could only be one winner. Despite Elizabeth's assertion of having 'the heart and stomach of a king' she had never led her men personally into battle like Granuaile nor, despite her claim to be 'mistress of the seas', had ever sailed further downriver than Greenwich. Elizabeth ruled from the protection and comfort of her palaces, surrounded by a retinue of loyal and able advisers. Granuaile fearlessly led and ruled by land and sea alone. Granuaile had taken two husbands and, if tradition is to be believed, at least one lover. She had borne three sons and a daughter. Elizabeth had retained her power only at the expense of personal happiness and fulfilment as a woman. Marriage had become incompatible with her crown, as she told Robert Dudley, one of the first of her many suitors,

'God's death, my lord, I will have but one mistress and no master.'[18]

Only in solitary virginity could Elizabeth hope to rule her bickering courtiers by appearing as a lover to them all and as a mother to her country. Granuaile had had it all.

On a summer's day in late July somewhere within the lavish surroundings of Greenwich palace these two elderly women came face to face. Their conversation was believed to have been conducted in Latin, the language often used by the English in their dealings with Irish chieftains and in which the Queen was one of the most proficient of her age. As befitted the occasion, Granuaile would undoubtedly have dressed with as much, if not more care, as she had in 1581, at Sir Nicholas Malby's celebrations in Galway, where she had been singled out among the other guests as being 'no small lady'. She could not, and perhaps wisely on this occasion chose not, to compete with Elizabeth in the fashion stakes. What was the advantage to be gained from such a display? Far better to achieve what she came for by evoking the Queen's compassion rather than her resentment. It was a successful ploy and one which paid dividends, because Elizabeth later urged Bingham 'to have pity for the poor aged woman,'[18] who had come before her, blithely ignoring the fact that they were of a similar age.

The correspondence emanating from the meeting is the only clue remaining to what transpired between the two women. Granuaile, in a later letter to Lord Burghley, writes of 'the clemencie and favour,'[20] displayed by the Queen towards her at their meeting. It is the Queen's letter regarding the meeting which is the more revealing and is testimony to how well Granuaile negotiated her case. The only unlawful act attributed to Granuaile during the course of the interview was her flamboyant chastisement of her son, Murrough-ne-Maor O'Flaherty, by which the Queen and Burghley seemed to have been amazed, as both mention the incident in their respective correspondence. The Queen glances over Granuaile's other more damning activities by referring merely that Granuaile 'hath at times lived out of order.'[21] She listened with a mixture of admiration and compassion to Granuaile as she outlined the excesses of Sir Richard Bingham against her and her family. She listened and heard Granuaile, with some audacity, seek her protection from her own governor. Granuaile asked the Queen to procure the release of her son and half-brother. She asked for her own reinstatement to her trade of 'maintenance by land and sea,'[22] which she couched in such a way that Elizabeth would interpret, 'that she will fight in our quarrel with all the world',[23] in order to 'yeild to her some maintenance,' as the Queen subsequently wrote, 'for her living the rest of her old years.'[24]

Granuaile took her leave of the Queen, who promised to have her requests investigated and to give her her letter to Sir Richard Bingham. Like officialdom everywhere, certain procedures had to be complied with. The Queen ordered her Privy Council to seek an explanation from Sir Richard Bingham regarding his treatment of Granuaile and how her situation could be relieved. In a letter bristling with indignation and self-righteousness, Bingham declared his innocence and dared Granuaile

> 'to shew me instance of any one that ever I used violence against, havinge alwayes (I thancke the Lord) had that consideracion of christian dutye as I never sought any man's bloode otherwise then by course of her Maties. comon lawes to take away.'[25]

Outraged that the Queen and her Council should contemplate reinstating Granuaile and Sir Murrough-ne-Doe, both of whom he had gone to such lengths to destroy, he contended, perhaps not without some semblance of truth, that

> ...for so long as Grany Ne Maly and he were of power to make any sturres the state was never troubled with their complaints but now that they are pulled dowen and forced in speight of their hartes to submit themselves to her Ma.ts lawes they pretend many wronges and are not ashamed to aske recompence .[26]

Rather than reinstating Granuaile and despite

> ...how great soever any may make her wich knoweth her not,I will never aske but a boat of xxx tonnes to beate her.. and with gods assistance dryve her and all her fleet into the sea.[27]

Burghley digested the intemperate tones of Bingham's letter before making final recommendations to the Queen. Meanwhile Granuaile remained in London, awaiting her response and fearing that Bingham might execute Tibbot-ne-Long in her absence. In early September, she wrote to Burghley reminding him that 'hir Matie hath promised hir hir letters to Sr Richard Bingham', and begging him to ensure that her 'sonne maye take no harme in body or goods untyll her Matie pleasure be further knowne.'[28] Eventually towards the end of September, Granuaile achieved her goal. The Queen wrote her recommendations to Bingham. She ordered the release of Tibbot-ne-Long and Dónal-ne-Piopa from prison. Regarding Granuaile's personal plight, which Elizabeth described as 'having not by the custom of the Irish any title to any livelihood or position or portion of her two husbands lands, now being a widow,'[29] she ordered that provision be made for Granuaile out of her sons' estates, the amount to be deducted, by the Queen's specific command, from their taxes. She urged Bingham 'that you also shall with your favour in all their good causes protect them to live in peace to enjoy their livelihoods'. She further noted that Granuaile had

> 'departeth with great thankfulness and with many more earnest promises that she will, as long as she lives, continue a dutiful subject, yea and will employ all her power to offend and prosecute any offender against Us,'[30]

a promise that, knowing Granuaile's capabilities and the opportunities that such an offer presented to her once back in Ireland, must have sent shivers of apprehension through Bingham.

*Left:*
*English Military*
*Tactics in 16th*
*century Ireland.*
*(Derrick, 1581)*

*Below:*
*Gaelic Chiefs*
*Submit to Sir*
*Henry Sidney.*
*(Derrick, 1581)*

*Howth Castle, County Dublin. (Private Collection)*

*Carraigahowley (Rockfleet) Castle. (Dúchas The Heritage Service)*

*Left:*
*Meeting of*
*Granuaile and*
*Queen Elizabeth I.*
*(National Library*
*of Ireland)*

*Below:*
*Facsimile of*
*Granuaile's Petition*
*to Elizabeth I.*
*(Public Record*
*Office, London)*

*Maude Bourke (b.1642) great–great–granddaughter of Granuaile.
(Westport House)*

*Bill signed by Maude Bourke (Browne) 1674. (Westport House)*

*Left:*
*Sir Richard Bingham,*
*Governor of Connaught.*
*(Private collection)*

*Below:*
*Westport House.*
*(Private Collection)*

*Above:*
*Sir William Cecil,*
*Lord Burghley.*
*(Private collection)*

*Right:*
*Thomas (Black Tom),*
*10th Earl of Ormond.*
*(Private collection)*

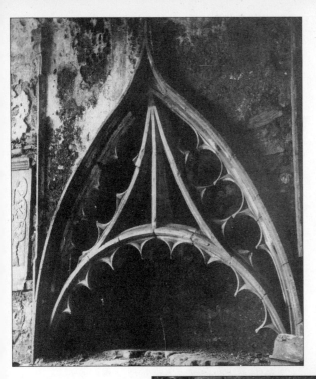

*Traditional Resting Place of Granuaile, Clare Island Abbey. (Dúchas The Heritage Service)*

*Stone Plaque, Clare Island Abbey. (Dúchas the Heritage Service)*

*Left:*
*Bronze Sculpture, Granuaile,*
*Westport House. (Michael*
*Cooper, FRBS)*

*Below:*
*Mary Robinson, former*
*President of Ireland and Anne*
*Chambers at the opening of the*
*Granuaile Visitor Centre,*
*Louisburgh, 1995. (Private*
*Collection)*

# CHAPTER NINE

# End of an Era

Granuaile's visit to the court of Elizabeth must have been the subject of much interest and discussion among her relations and followers in Connaught. That she could negotiate with an authority greater than the seemingly omnipotent English governor who held the Gaelic leaders of the province in his grip, and successfully have his dictates over-ruled, undoubtedly added greatly to her prestige among them. That she likewise made an impression on the queen and her ministers is evidenced by their entertainment of her in the first place and by their investigation of her requests. Her status as a political leader in Ireland was further confirmed in the new map of Ireland by Baptista Boazio, published a few years later, where her name figures prominently among the listed Irish chieftains – the only woman included. What the Irish annalists chose to conceal and ignore, English cartographers and administrators were more willing to concede – Granuaile had earned the right to be numbered among the leaders of sixteenth-century Ireland, as valid a chieftain as any of her male peers.

The practical results of her mission to England took longer to manifest themselves. Bingham proved recalcitrant to act upon instructions, even when confronted with the provisions of the queen's letter, which Granuaile delivered to him personally. But Granuaile was not prepared to allow her endeavours regarding her son and her half-brother to be negated by Bingham's hostility. She threatened Bingham that if he did not accede to the queen's instructions, as Bingham wrote, 'importunately swearing that she would else repair againe into England'.[1] Eventually with great reluctance he agreed to 'enlarge Grany O'Mally, her son Tibbot and brother Donel na Pippe, upon such slender surytes (sureties).'[2]

Bingham realised the Irishwoman had pulled a fast one on his queen, who, in acceding to her requests, had neglected to obtain the usual sureties or pledges in lieu of favours or granted. Pardons and favours usually cost, but Granuaile had extracted them from the Queen free gratis. Elizabeth and Burghley had underestimated the capabilities of the 'aged woman', whose age belied the boundless energy and plotting talents that had helped her survive for so long. But Bingham had first-hand experience of Granuaile's capabilities as a determined and cunning foe. He realised that the queen had in effect granted his most persistent adversary a *carte blanche* to return to sea with her galleys and resume her old trade of 'maintenance', under the guise of fighting the queen's 'quarrel with all the world', despite all he had expended and endured to destroy her. For the moment, there was little he could do but obey the queen's command and await to get his own back on his adversary.

Bingham freed Tibbot-ne-Long from prison in Athlone in late September 1593. Tibbot-ne-Long wrote later of the deprivation he had endured while in Bingham's custody and stated that, 'he could not stand upon his legges through that durance and misery he suffered there.'[3] Granuaile's step-brother, Dónal-ne-Piopa, was also released. With both of them free from Bingham's clutches, Granuaile busied herself to take full advantage of the queen's letter regarding her own situation. To this effect, she started to rebuild her fleet for the purpose of re-establishing her trade of 'maintenance' by sea, with three large galleys, which English records describe as being capable of carrying three hundred men apiece. The countryside around still bore the scars of warfare, and the sea was once again to be her salvation. Bingham watched her preparations with alarm as he searched for a way of thwarting her without openly disobeying the orders of his queen.

Just as Granuaile prepared to return to the sea, furnished with her newly acquired galleys, Bingham struck back. Contrary to the conditions of the Composition, he ordered a Captain Strittes and a troop of soldiers to accompany her by sea to monitor her activities and pressed her and her ships into service against her own kinsmen. He forced her and Tibbot-ne-Long, as she later complained to England, 'to repair to the seas wher in certain illandes eighteen chiefest of the Bourkes being proclaimed traytors were killed.'[4] These were the remnants of the army of her grandson, Richard Bourke, the son of the Devil's Hook, who, acting as a decoy for O'Neill and Maguire in Ulster, had plundered north Mayo but had been routed by a detachment of Bingham's troops. They then had subsequently been attacked by the Bourkes of Erris. Richard Bourke and others had taken refuge on the lonely island of Iniskea, off Achill, where the massacre took place. Richard Bourke and four of his companions managed to escape. To be party to the slaughter of their relations must have been a bitter pill for Granuaile to swallow. Their involuntary co-operation was later given as proof of Tibbot-ne-Long's loyalty to the queen by certain officers in the English service, anxious to lure him to the English side and away from confederacy with the Ulster chieftains. It is highly unlikely, however, that they did so voluntarily, as Granuaile's son-in-law, the Devil's Hook, and his son, Richard Bourke, continued to be Granuaile's, and later Tibbot-ne-Long's most steadfast allies. Tibbot-ne-Long's later campaign in April 1595 against the Bourkes of Erris, where he killed a number of their leaders, under the guise of service to the Crown, was in reality to revenge their attack on his kinsmen in 1593.

To curb Granuaile from further plotting against him by land, Bingham caused a detachment of his soldiers to

> place and cesse themselves taking up meat and drinke after their own serving and six pens per diem for every souldier and four pens per diem for his mann, where they do remain all these seaven moneths...[5]

on her lands. The result of such an onerous demand on her depleted resources was, as Granuaile vividly described to Burghley, the impoverishment of herself, her son, cousins and followers.

Unable to bear the financial strain, Granuaile, her son, cousins and followers were forced to flee Mayo and 'to withdraw themselves into the province of Mounster, where they do remain in great distress.'[6] We can envisage this exodus from Mayo – the little band of refugees, whose only hope of salvation lay in the dauntlessness and the contacts of the remarkable, elderly matriarch who had been their leader for forty years. Their faith in her limitless energy, political acumen and sheer nerve must have been great to risk such a journey. They sailed from Clew Bay southwards, rounded the south coast and up the river Suir where, in April 1595, Granuaile again sought the help of Black Tom, Earl of

Ormond, at his newly built Elizabethan manor at Carrick-on-Suir. She prevailed on the powerful earl, as he wrote to Burghley,

> for my letter to you on her behalf as I could not refrain to write these fewe lines unto your Lordship by her. Though I was verie lothe considering your Ls. Weightie causes to trouble you with her private suite, the declaration whereof I refer to herself...[7]

Black Tom persuaded Granuaile in her accompanying petition to tender submissions again to the queen concerning the lands of both her sons – Tibbot-ne-Long and Murrough-ne-Maor O'Flaherty – as well as the land of her O'Malley relations who had fled south in her company. To alleviate their desperate plight, she sought again a means to circumvent Bingham's close scrutiny of her activities at sea, which was rendering her both powerless and penniless. She offered the queen to

> to serve with a hundred men at her owne charges at seas upon the coaste of Ireland in her Majesties warres uponn all occasions from Easter to Michelmas...[8]

The idea of this very old (by the standards of the day) woman, still an active leader of an army of 100 men and a fleet of ships, and able to engage in warfare is, from a mere physical perspective, quite simply unique. The strategy behind the offer she makes the queen is testament to a mind that is sharp and calculating, unaffected by the passing years. While her offer was not immediately availed of by the Privy Council, it acted later as a means by which her sons, were accorded the leadership of such a private army, formerly in their mother's pay but then paid for out of the queen's purse.

From Black Tom's letter and from a later petition, dated 5 May 1595, from Granuaile to Burghley, in which she refers to 'at my last beinge here'[9] (at the English court), it is clear that some time between 17 April, the date of Black Tom's covering letter, and 5 May, she sailed again to England to plead her case, this time with Lord Burghley. Unlike the formality of her earlier petitions, which are written mainly in the third person, this petition is written in the first person. In it Granuaile informs Burghley that because of 'Sir Richard Binghams hard dealinge'[10] of her, and contrary to the earlier provision made for her by the queen, she had been unable to 'posses and injoie the third parte of the lands and comodities of McWilliam and Oflahertie as lawful wif unto each of them...'[11] She begged him to make Bingham back off so that, as she says:

> I may lyve secure of my life which hath been attempted sundrie tmes be the said Sr Richard Bingham his brethren and others by his direcsion...[12]

She asked 'for the Lord Treasurer's favourable letters in me owne and me sonnes behalf to the Lo. Deputie and to Sr Richard Bingham,' and craved his lordship's pardon 'for my contynuall boldness'. Her 'boldness' was rewarded when, in August 1595, a commission was granted by the queen and the Privy Council to investigate the lands in Mayo claimed by her sons, Tibbot-ne-Long and Murrough O'Flaherty, her grandson, Dónal O'Flaherty, son of Owen, Owen, Dermot and Dónal O'Malley of 'Owel O'Maillie', and Miles MacEvilly, Tibbot-ne-Long's foster-father 'with the intention of the Queen accepting their surrenders of the premises and regranting them by letters patent...'[13]

Regarding her own harsh treatment at the hands of Bingham, fate was about to intervene to remove him once and for all from Connaught. Burghley's entertainment of her petition and his intervention again with the queen are testimony to Granuaile's intuitive persistence and to her ability to have her case heard by those in power in England, rather than suffer the indignity of having to seek favours from unfriendly and less influential administrators in Ireland. But favours had to be reciprocated, and from the time of this, her final visit to court, a marked shift began to emerge in her allegiance and that of her sons.

By mid-1595, Hugh O'Neill, the Earl of Tyrone, had shed all semblance of loyalty to the crown and had sent his brother, Art, to attack and capture the English garrison fort on the Blackwater, which Tyrone had earlier helped the English to build. It was a clear statement that his previous protestations of loyalty were but a stalling tactic. A unique and formidable confederacy spear-headed by O'Neill and his less cautious ally, Red Hugh O'Donnell, was being shaped from out of the traditional whirlpool of Gaelic disunity. In their despatches to the Spanish court, O'Neill and O'Donnell now represented their cause for the first time as an 'Irish' one. They offered the 'crown of Ireland' to Philip, 'if he would deliver them from their English oppressors.'[14] But, as ever, personal vendettas and individual power struggles threatened the confederacy from the start. Nowhere else was this more blatantly apparent than in Mayo, where O'Donnell's aggression was to alienate Granuaile and her sons from the Ulster confederacy.

The O'Donnell's of Tirconail had traditionally claimed over-lordship of north Mayo – a claim that had ever been forcibly resisted by the Bourkes and their allies. To secure a passage into Connaught, Red Hugh O'Donnell sought to reactivate that claim. In June 1595, Sligo Castle, regarded as the key to the defence of Connaught, was captured and given to O'Donnell, affording him an unhindered passage into Mayo. To demonstrate the extent of his power to the, as yet unaligned chieftains of Mayo, O'Donnell looted and plundered throughout the county. The Mayo chieftains were caught between two opposing forces, Bingham and O'Donnell, and felt the brunt of both, as one observer reported:

> Through the fear the people have of Sir Richard Bingham, their necessity drives them to depend on O'donnell, whom they hate for his pride and ambition and are weary of the burdens he daily lays upon them.[15]

However, Bingham's days as governor were numbered. A new conspiracy among his fellow administrators was afoot to remove him from office. Fearing that the charges were stacked against him, Bingham fled to England in September and was promptly imprisoned. Sir Conyers Clifford was appointed governor in his place.

O'Donnell pushed home his advantage in Mayo, and the chieftains there had little option but to bow to his demands. Granuaile and Tibbot-ne-Long, had little option but bear the harsh exactions he imposed. The new English governor, Sir Conyers Clifford, also sought their allegiance. He met with Tibbot-ne-Long, who, displaying the calculation and cunning that were to stand him well over the coming traumatic years, for a while succeeded in playing one side off against the other with commendable skill. The English in Connaught well realised his worth. Because of the slaying in August of his half-brother, Edmund Bourke, as he attempted to escape from Galway gaol, Tibbot-ne-Long had emerged as the most powerful leader in the Bourke hierarchy. His power, particularly by sea, which because of the disturbed and desolate state of Mayo was regarded as an indispensable asset to both sides in the conflict, made him a formidable ally or foe. For Granuaile, the removal of Bingham was an answer to all that she had sought, and at the remarkable age of sixty-five years she was free to return to her career of 'maintenance' by sea.

In December 1595 an event occurred which was to shape the future political direction taken by Granuaile and Tibbot-ne-Long. It centred, as it had for Tibbot's father and generations of Bourkes before him, on the contentious and still seductive issue of the MacWilliamship. Rampant in Mayo, O'Donnell announced is intention of reviving the title outlawed by the English. In late December, all the Bourke septs of Mayo made their way to their ancient inaugural site at Rousakeera. O'Donnell arrived with an army and with many of his Ulster client chieftains. Blatantly and with great insensitivity, he physically excluded the Bourkes from their ancient ceremony and imposed a MacWilliam of his own choosing, Theobald, son of Walter Ciotach of Tirawley, the least eligible of the Bourke candidates. The selection was received with uproar by the Bourke septs. O'Donnell's hopes of Bourke allegiance against the English were decidedly weakened by his rashness and lack of judgement:

> Hitherto the old customs were the alternative to the Queen's government. Now, the choice was between the Queen's government and the old customs subject to the very heavy burden of O'Donnell's domination.[16]

To ensure that the principal contenders for the MacWilliamship would not serve against him, O'Donnell took hostages with him back to Tirconail, including Tibbot-ne-Long. In the event, O'Donnell's MacWilliam failed to command the allegiance of most of the Bourke septs and was eventually driven out of Mayo.

With Bingham out of the picture, Granuaile busied herself again by sea. The lands of her son, out of which the queen had granted her maintenance, had been repeatedly ravaged by O'Donnell and his MacWilliam, and were once again desolate. Back on the sea she raided and plundered south and north. Her ships were reported operating off the coast of Thomond, where the Earl of Thomond was forced to do battle with some of her followers who had landed in search of plunder. In 1596 the Dean of Limerick, writing to the English council, reported that 'Grany ny Maly and Mac Neil of Barra invaded one anothers possessions though farre distant...'[17] The fact that she was prepared and able to sail in a retaliatory mission to the Isle of Barra, off the coast of Scotland, is testimony to her great endurance. The sea took a heavy toll of life and health. Few seamen in the sixteenth century lived to such an advanced age. Fewer still could physically operate in such a demanding and dangerous environment, as Granuaile continued to do until the close of the century. Like most of her contemporaries she was powerless to avert the oncoming mayhem as every leader became sucked into the maw of the final futile struggle of Gaelic Ireland, led by O'Neill and O'Donnell, to win back lost ground and reinstate itself against the determined onslaught of England. Survival was now her single purpose.

The effects of O'Donnell's actions against the Bourkes did not take long to manifest themselves. On his escape from O'Donnell's custody, Tibbot-ne-Long returned to Mayo, which was devastated by O'Donnell's raids. In February 1597, the English governor, Sir Conyers Clifford, took up duty in Connaught. His style of government differed greatly from Bingham's as he sought to attain the allegiance of the chieftains by conciliatory measures, rather than by force. He had already become acquainted with Tibbot-ne-Long's brother-in-law, Donough O'Connor Sligo, at the English court. On his arrival in Connaught, Clifford immediately rewarded that friendship by recapturing Sligo Castle and reinstating O'Connor Sligo. Well satisfied with the outcome, O'Connor Sligo then 'established friendship and concord between his brother-in-law, Theobald-ne-Long...and Sir Conyers Clifford.'[18] Tibbot-ne-Long, together with Richard Bourke, the Devil's Hook's son, O'Malley, MacJordan and others agreed to terms with Clifford. They were pardoned of all past 'offences' and provided with cattle. In return, they agreed to pay the arrears of the Composition rent outstanding, support the governor and hand over pledges for their loyalty. Together with his new-found allies, Tibbot-ne-Long marched into Tirawley and as the *Annals of the Four Masters* recorded, 'expelled and banished MacWilliam...to O'Donnell...The Country generally on this occasion adhered to Tibóid-ne-Long and the Governor.'[19]

With most of Mayo siding with him, and the with Ulster confederacy growing in strength, Tibbot-ne-Long fully realised his worth to the English, and put a price on his continuing loyalty. On 25 April 1597, he presented the governor with a set of fourteen demands for the continuation of his service. Clifford sent the demands to the Privy Council for deliberation. The outcome was that Tibbot-ne-Long secured the extensive lands of the MacWilliamship and a title. (The title was not granted until 1627 when Tibbot-ne-Long was created the first Viscount Mayo by Charles I.) He was granted the lands of those within his own sept who had been killed in rebellion. He received a company of foot soldiers in the queen's pay. He secured pardons for his half-brother, his ally, Richard

Bourke, for whom he also secured a pension, his mother's half-brother, Dónal-na-Piopa, and others of his relations. To ensure his control over the septs of Mayo, he sought a commission to grant protections, a demand which was, however, mitigated. The document served as a basis by which, over the coming years of political and social upheaval and displacement, Tibbot-ne-Long emerged as the largest land-owner in Mayo. His rise marked the decay of the Gaelic tribal system and the emergence of English civil law in Ireland.

From the English records which survive, it appears that Granuaile backed and profited from her son's arrangement with the English authorities. In August 1597 Clifford indicated to the lord deputy that he had 'given him [Tibbot-ne-long], his mother and brother amongst them in money and other necessaries, £200',[20] for their services by sea.

Perhaps it is their actions in the final years of the sixteenth century that deleted Granuaile and to a lesser extent her son from the history books. Patriotism was not applicable to sixteenth-century Ireland. Granuaile's actions and those of her sons were guided primarily by the struggle to survive. Physical survival against the power of the sea and the elements was undoubtedly Granuaile's first challenge. Survival by sea must have made the political obstacles she encountered during her lifetime seem insignificant by comparison. But the goal was the same. When her political strategy is examined within the context of her time, she emerges as a realist. Survival was the spur for any Gaelic leader either to resist the encroachment of individual English administrators, or to accept the changes to whatever degree would guarantee survival. The idea of a common enemy, and the creation of a united front by which to oppose him, only became an issue very late in the century; and for people like Granuaile and her sons, too late. We must look to later centuries when patriotism and nationalism became the spur for resistance and rebellion.

While opposing individual English administrators like Bingham when they impinged directly on her power, Granuaile's fight was not against the English or for the Irish. And this was the accepted face of Irish politics in the sixteenth century. Although to the generations of historians who came after her the political manipulations of Granuaile might lack the obligatory patriotic gloss, the fact that her status as a political leader in Gaelic society was not diminished, but rather augmented, by her association with elements in the English administration, is sufficient proof of the appropriateness of her strategy.

As the revolt of the Ulster chieftains gathered momentum and spilled over into Mayo, the advantages won by Tibbot-ne-Long from the English took some years to materialise. O'Donnell and his MacWilliam repeatedly raided Mayo, giving those who opposed them little chance to recover. When, on 14 August 1598, the English were overwhelmed by the forces of O'Neill and O'Donnell at the Battle of the Yellow Ford, many of the Connaught chieftains who had stood aloof or who had aligned with the English governor, changed sides. Now virtually unopposed, O'Donnell raided at will through Mayo and Galway down to Thomond. In the autumn, he sent his MacWilliam and O'Doherty specifically to plunder Granuaile's territory around Murrisk and Burrishoole. The incident was enshrined in the line of a contemporary poem:

> *Gráinne na gCearbhach do creach*
> (Grace of the Gamblers he plundered)

It referred to her known penchant for gambling with the

gaming dice, although in this instance, with the political dice, but it is also an interesting acknowledgement as to her continuing status as a political figure.

Now almost seventy, and in her declining years, Granuaile must surely have left her struggle with the sea and with the world in the capable hands of her sons. While their activities and the part they played in the concluding years of the century are well documented, there are few additional references to the activities of Granuaile. One of the final recorded notices of her appeared in the state papers in July 1601, in a despatch from the captain of an English warship. It is fittingly enough an account of his encounter with one of her galleys sailing on a mission of plunder:

> All the sails I have seen since I came upon the coast was a galley I met withal betwixt Teelin and Killibegs, where I made her run on shore among the rocks, notwithstanding she rowed with thirty oars and had on board ready to defend her 100 good shot, which entertained skirmish with my boat and had put her to the worst. But coming up with my ship to her rescue, I quickly with my great shot made an end to the fray. This galley comes out of Connaught and belongs to Grace O'Malley…this with one other galley was set out and manned with a people called the Flaherties who was proposed to do some spoils upon the countries of MacSwyne Fanad and MacSwyne ne Doe about Lough Swilly and Sheephaven…[21]

That Granuaile was still alive appears likely and, while not actively involved in this particular incident, it seems that under her direction her trade of 'maintenance by land and sea' was being continued by her followers.

Thus the extraordinary life of Granuaile ends as it begins

– shrouded in uncertainty. The exact date of her death, as of her birth, is uncertain. From the evidence to hand, it appears that her death occurred at Carraigahowley Castle about 1603. She probably survived to hear of the defeat of O'Neill and O'Donnell at the battle of Kinsale, the final and conclusive milestone in the long and bloody struggle between the Gaelic world of her birth and the new world of her sons' adoption. Perhaps she also lived to hear of the death in March 1603 of Queen Elizabeth, her adversary and her benefactor. Tradition holds that she is buried in the ruins of the Cisterian abbey on Clare Island, an appropriate resting place for a Sea Queen.

While denied a place in the annals and histories of Ireland, Granuaile's memory remained alive among the people in the area where she once lived. The English also had good reason to remember her long after her death. Writing in 1623, the then English lord deputy, seeking to justify the seizure of fishing rights on the borders of Mayo and Galway, reminded the Privy Council, that the inhabitants of Mayo:

> have been always more apt to rebellion than any in that kingdom in soe much that the very women have borne armes there, whereof Grany ne Maly was famous and is yett renowned by them...[22]

In the west of Ireland her stone fortresses stand solidly still in remembrance of their audacious chatelaine. Her main abode, Carraigahowley, stands stark and brooding, the sea waves lapping gently at its stone walls. Across the bay on Clare Island the ruins of 'Grania's castle' evoke images of the Pirate Queen.

More recently, her story has fired the imagination in a wide range of creative disciplines, and her life has been depicted in fiction, music, dance, documentary and film. She has become the inspiration for women's self-awareness groups, both in Ireland and abroad, for yacht races and diving clubs named in her honour. A new interpretative centre depicting her life and times was opened by Her Excellency, Mary Robinson, President of Ireland, in Louisburgh on the shores of Clew Bay. Skilled craftsmen at Waterford Glass encapsulated the essence of her seafaring life in a unique study in the famed Irish crystal, for presentation to the people of Clare Island. The modern-day O'Malley clan, its members scattered throughout the world, have come together each year since 1953 to commemorate and celebrate their remarkable antecedent. The Granuaile Trust, founded by the clan, helps to develop projects in the cultural and environmental fields. Named in her honour, the newly built ferry, *The Pirate Queen*, brings visitors to Clare Island to view her castle and final resting place, while the Irish Lights vessel, *The Granuaile*, keeps a watching brief on the coasts once traversed by this intrepid seafarer.

But it is the swirls and flourishes on the parchment manuscripts of the sixteenth-century English state papers, the letters, despatches and memorabilia of the Tudor conquest of Ireland, that have preserved for posterity the tantalising character and career of Granuaile and the impact she made on that traumatic era. These relics, now brittle and faded with age, challenge our predisposed sense of convention, our assumptions regarding what is possible, and rip apart the shallow boundaries that society tends to impose on women – boundaries which Granuaile, by 'overstepping the part of womanhood', dared to breach. Above all, they allow us a glimpse of one of the greatest survivors of them all.

# CHAPTER TEN

# The Descendants of Granuaile

Granuaile left her struggle with the world in the capable hands of her two sons, Murrough-ne-Maor O'Flaherty and Tibbot-ne-Long Bourke. Both were to prove as able as their indomitable mother in the art of survival. Pragmatic and ambitious, both possessed the traits of compromise and cunning that, as the sixteenth century drew to its inevitably traumatic close, were the essential weapons necessary to make it into the new century. Of similar outlook and character, they tended to operate in tandem and, as well as being blood-related, they became close political allies. Although the older, Murrough-ne-Maor seemed content to be directed by his younger more influential half-brother and lived to reap the rewards. Their lives are a unique commentary on a period of fundamental transition and change in Ireland. Theirs is the story of the minor chieftains who at the close of the sixteenth century occupied the middle ground between the fixed battlelines of two incompatible protagonists, trapped by events outside their control. Many became pawns in a momentous game of strategy. Others, like the sons of Granuaile, 'plotted their own moves and in a game within a game, became intrepid knights charting their own survival.'[1]

Initially it was their seapower and seafaring expertise
which they inherited from their mother, combined with the
undoubted following they both enjoyed within their
territories, that made them much sought after by the
opposing sides. Both were allied, by August 1597, ostensibly
with the English governor against O'Donnell. In the last
years leading up to Kinsale, as the balance of power shifted
in Connaught between Clifford and O'Donnell, they flirted
with both sides, to the utter consternation of the English
administrators. 'I know not of one day's service that Tibbot
ne Longe hath performed,'[2] the Machiavellian president of
Munster, Sir George Carew, complained to the Privy
Council.

> 'Tibbott ne Longe was within with O'Donnell and
> O'Donnell did send out of him as pledges...the best of
> his country. Tyrone himself say they are agreed, but
> they will not have any know of it,'[3] a spy reported to the
> Earl of Essex in 1599.

There was one issue guaranteed to make Tibbot-ne-Long
act unambiguously. This was the vexed question of the
MacWilliamship, which right to the close of the century was
to continue to be the divisive issue it had always been and
continued to arouse in him the same emotive response as it
had in his ancestors. Even when his erstwhile English ally
Clifford was attacked and killed in the Battle of the Curlew
mountains in 1599, it was the issue of the MacWilliamship
that kept Tibott-ne-Long from finally throwing in his lot
with O'Donnell. The lands pertaining to the title rather
than the title itself were now the magnet. As Tibbot-ne-
Long well realised the MacWilliamship would never again,
no matter which side emerged victorious in the coming
confrontation, attain its original prestige. In his deal with

the English, the Privy Council had conferred him with part of the MacWilliamship estate and he had already moved with his family inland to Belcarra Castle. In 1600 on his return from a stint of dubious duty in Munster, ostensibly leading an army in the Queen's pay, he expelled O'Donnell's MacWilliam who, in his absence, had come into Mayo. Pressed by Sir Henry Docwra who had landed behind his lines in Lough Foyle and by his rival, Niall Grav O'Donnell, Red Hugh O'Donnell could no longer support his MacWilliam. Now unopposed in Mayo, Tibbot-ne-Long convened a meeting of all the Bourke septs at Rousakeera and conferred the MacWilliamship on his longtime ally, Granuaile's grandson, Richard Bourke, the son of the Devil's Hook.

To confer the MacWilliamship on a subordinate rather than to assume the title himself was a shrewd move. Tibbot already possessed most of the lands and privileges pertaining to the title. If he was to maintain credence with the English, he could not be seen to assume a proscribed office. Moreover, by conferring the title on a lesser chieftain, he demonstrated that he had become, in effect, greater than the once all-powerful MacWilliam. The final struggle for the ancient title in itself symbolised the final struggle being waged by the Gaelic world that had bred and sustained it through the centuries. Perhaps it was the inevitability of the decline of the MacWilliamship that made Tibbot-ne-Long refuse to be the last holder of a doomed office or the champion of the doomed world that it represented.

On 23 September 1601, Spanish troops under the command of Don Juan del'Aquila arrived to support the Ulster chieftains against the English. They landed, however, at Kinsale in the southernmost part of the country. The entire length of Ireland lay between them and their allies,

O'Neill and O'Donnell in Ulster. In late October the Spaniards were besieged by an army, ostensibly English but in reality composed of as many Irish, commanded by Lord Mountjoy. In Ulster Red Hugh O'Donnell quickly mustered his army and in an incredible feat of endurance and military genius, outmarched and outmanoeuvred the English forces sent to bar his way to Kinsale. At the end of November his more cautious ally, Hugh O'Neill, also made the long journey south. With a combined army of 6,000, they besieged the besiegers. At the beginning of December, leading an army of 300, Tibbot-ne-Long marched out of Mayo and also headed south. As he approached Kinsale, neither Mountjoy nor O'Neill knew with certainty on which side he intended to fight. At Kinsale, after months of vacillation, Tibbot-ne-Long finally showed his hand and fought alongside the victorious Mountjoy.

After Kinsale a new war for possession of the land of Ireland commenced. Despite the defeat at Kinsale, at the beginning of the seventeenth century, the greater part of the land of Ireland was still in Gaelic hands. With the collapse of the Gaelic system and the Flight of the Earls in 1607, vast areas were open to the lust for land of a new wave of English planters, adventurers and entrepreneurs, armed with vague and suspect titles to the properties of Gaelic chieftains. In this new war, waged with maps, quill and parchment, inquisitions and legal rhetoric, Tibbot-ne-Long's instinct for survival endured its greatest test in the battle for the land of Mayo. For the space of three decades he successfully competed within the framework of an alien legal system and increased his patrimony substantially, despite the Crown's suspicions and against the concerted efforts of the many English adventurers and speculators who sought to deny him. By mortgage, purchase, claim and counter-claim, by right both of Gaelic and English law, Tibbot-ne-Long amassed the largest estate in Mayo, mostly at the expense of his less well-off and legally astute relations, in particular the O'Malleys, various septs of the Bourkes and his foster family, the MacEvillys of Carra. After Kinsale he abandoned his seafaring activities to consolidate his position on land. The remains of his mother's fleet continued to be operated by her O'Malley relations into the middle of the new century but without the effectiveness or flamboyance of Granuaile.

Tibbot-ne-Long was knighted by the new king of England, James 1 on 4 January 1603 in recognition of his 'loyal and valorous' service. He was styled Sir Tibbot (ne Longe) Bourke. The letters patent relating to his enoblement were preserved in Westport House. They are written in Latin on six pages of fine parchment and are hand-coloured with the De Burgo arms, Tibbot-ne-Long's personal arms and a portrait of King James 1. In 1627 he was created Viscount Mayo by Charles I. Despite his royal honours, however, the English never shed their suspicions about his loyalty. Until his death at Kinturk Castle in 1629, he continued to scheme and intrigue with exiled elements of the Gaelic resistance that he had fought against at Kinsale and endured imprisonment and investigation in the process. But being the survivor that he was, he managed to retain both his head and his newly-acquired lands and titles and, paradoxically, the esteem and loyalty of his Gaelic followers and neighbours. He is buried in Ballintubber abbey.

Murrough-ne-Maor predeceased his half-brother by three years. He died at Bunowen Castle in April 1626 and was buried, according to his wishes, in the Abbey of St Francis in Galway, the city from whence his ancestors had been debarred. In his will, by which he appointed Tibbot-ne-Long his executor, he provided for each of his eight sons and two daughters out of his large estate which stretched from Bunowen, north to Renvyle and south to Kilkieran. One of the stipulations of his will was the provision for

> 'my fifth son Patricke who is become a scholler, £20 when he is ready and determined to goe beyond the seas to studie, together with £10, everie year during his continuance beyond the seas.'[4]

His eldest son, known as Murrough-na-Mart, (of the Beeves) succeeded him and was knighted by the Lord Deputy, Sir Thomas Wentworth, in 1637. He was subsequently dispossessed of his estates by the Cromwellian confiscations in 1653 and his descendants were gradually reduced to the status of impoverished farmers.

The descendants of Granuaile through the marriage of her daughter Margaret O'Flaherty to Richard Bourke, the Devil's Hook, are unknown, as are also her O'Flaherty descendants through her eldest son, Owen.

Tibbot-nc-Long's death notice was registered at Athlone Castle. The entry reads:

> The right Honorable sr Theobald Burke Kt viscount Burke of Mayo, deceased the 18 June 1629. He had to wife maude, dr of Charles O'Connor Sligoe, by whome he had issue, the right Ho. Miles, Viscount Burke, David, Theobald, Richard, Mary, Onore and Margaret...[5]

His eldest son Miles, perhaps named in honour of Tibbot-ne-Long's foster father Miles MacEvilly, whose lands and castles of Kinturk, Kilboynell (afterwards Castlebourke) and Manulla were by now subsumed into his estate, became the second Viscount Mayo. Like his father he endured the continuing distrust of the English establishment and for a time was confined at the Gatehouse at Westminster. To hold on to his estates, he outwardly conformed to the reformed religion. He played a somewhat nefarious role in the massacre of Protestant settlers at Shrule in 1640. His son, Theobald, the third viscount, who made a valiant attempt to avert the slaughter, was subsequently tried, found guilty and executed by the Cromwellians, more with an eye to his confiscated estates than to his alleged involvement in the crime. Theobald, the fourth viscount, was regranted only part of his estates on the restoration of Charles II. By the time of the last acknowledged viscount, John Bourke, who died in 1767, the original Mayo estate so deftly put together by Tibbot-ne-Long, was reduced through confiscation and mortgage to Castlebourke and a few hundred acres of land.

On the death of the eighth Viscount Mayo, who was considered to have no male heir, the title officially lay dormant. There is much evidence to suggest that the title should not have been declared dormant but that on the death of the eighth viscount, a David Bourke, from Asgalan in the barony of Murrisk, a direct descendant of Richard, the fourth son of Tibbot-ne-long, was the rightful claimant. His claim was supported by the depositions of the sister of the eighth viscount, the dowager countess of the seventh viscount and many of the retainers and friends of the last deceased viscount. To the doctor who attended him on his deathbed in 1790, David Bourke, claimed to be the ninth Viscount Mayo. Richard Bourke, his uncle from Ballyhaunis, claimed as tenth viscount but had not the means to pursue his case through the courts. On his death, his son and heir, Michael Bourke of Lavalaroe, submitted additional sworn affidavits that he was 'the fourth cousin in

the male line of collateral descent to the late John, lord
Viscount Bourke of Mayo,'[6] but his claim, due to his meagre
means, was not successful and he died sometime after 1814.
The Viscount Mayo title was subsequently subsumed into
the Earldom of Mayo, a more recent creation.

The descendants of Granuaile are mainly traceable
through her Bourke line and her bloodline is to be found
among many pedigrees of both aristocrat and commoner.
Some of her descendants, like Granuaile herself, made an
impact on their age. Her great-great-great grandaughters
were Maria and Elizabeth Gunning, known as the 'gorgeous
Gunnings' from Castlecoote, County Roscommon. In the
eighteenth century they took English society by storm with
their beauty. One married the Earl of Coventry and
secondly the Duke of Hamilton; the other married the Duke
of Argyle.

In 1669, Granuaile's great-great-grandaughter, Maude
Bourke, daughter of Theobald the third Viscount Mayo,
married John Browne of Westport. Their mansion,
Westport House, was built near the old O'Malley fortress of
Cathair-na-Mart, where Dónal-na-Piopa, Granuaile's half-
brother, once resided. Westport House was the first stately
home in Ireland to open its doors to the public in 1961. It
has since become one of Ireland's premier tourist
attractions, having to-date welcomed over 2 million visitors.
The descendants of Maude Bourke and John Browne
continue to live of Westport House and the present owner,
Jeremy Browne, eleventh Marquess of Sligo, is thirteenth
great-grandson in descent from Granuaile. In the summer
of 2003, a life-size sculpture in bronze of Granuaile, by the
accomplished sculptor, Michael Cooper, was unveiled in the
grounds of Westport House.

Claiming a similar descent is the film producer, Lord John

Brabourne, married to the daughter of the late Lord Louis Mountbatten. With tragic perversity, their son, Nicholas, a fourteenth great-grandson in descent from Granuaile, was killed with his grandfather, grandmother and young friend off Mulloughmore harbour in Sligo in 1988, in waters once traversed by his remarkable ancestor.

The descendants through Granuaile's O'Malley relations, particularly her half-brother, Dónal-na-Piopa, are less certain. Confiscation, deprivation and famine scattered the clan O'Malley throughout the world. Tracing individual O'Malley family branches back as far as the sixteenth century and unravelling their connections to Granuaile, the passage of time and lack of authentic records, have made a difficult task. But O'Malleys everywhere can take pride in the fact that they originate from the same seafaring clan from the lordship of Umhall on the west coast of Ireland, and that they share a common heritage with the most famous member of the clan to bear the name O'Máille - Granuaile.

# Poems and Songs

### Granuaile

There stands a tower by the Atlantic side
A grey old tower, by storm and sea-waves beat
Perch'd on a cliff, beneath it yawneth wide
A lofty cavern of yore a fit retreat
For pirates galleys; altho', now, you'll meet
Nought but the seal and wild gull; from that cave
A hundred steps do upwards lead your feet
Unto a lonely chamber! -Bold and brave
Is he who climbs that stair, all slippery from the wave.

I sat there on an evening. In the west,
Amid the waters, sank the setting sun:
While clouds, like parting friends, about him prest,
Clad in their fleecy garbs, of gold and dun;
And silence was around me -save the hum,
Of the lone and wild bee, or the curlew's cry.
And lo! Upon me did a vision come,
Of her who built that tower, in days gone by;
And in that dream, behold! I saw a building high.

A stately hull-lofty and carved the roof -
Was deck'd with silken banners fair to see.
The hanging velvet, from Genou's woof,
And wrought with Tudor roses curiously;
At its far end did stand a canopy,
Shading a chair of state, on which was seen
A ladye fair, with look of majesty,
Amid a throng, 'yclad in costly sheen -
Nobles and gallant Knights proclaim her England's Queen.
The sage Elizabeth; and by her side

Were group'd her counsellors, with calm, grave air,
Burleigh and Walsingham, with others, tried
In wisdom and in war, and sparkling there,
Like Summer butterflies, were damsels fair,
Beautiful and young: behind a trusty band
Of stalwart yeomanry, with watchful care,
The portal guard, while nigher to its stand
Usher and page, ready to ape with willing hand.

A Tucket sounds, and lo! There enters now
A strange group, in saffron tunics drest:
A female at their head, whose step and brow
Herald her rank, and, calm and self possest,
Onward she came, alone through England's best,
With careless look, and bearing free yet high,
Tho' gentle dames their titterings scarce represt,
Noting her garments as she passed them by;
None laughed again who met that stern and flashing eye.

Restless and dark, its sharp and rapid look
Showd's a fierce spirit, prone a wrong to feel,
And quicker to revenge it. As a book.
That sun-burnt brow did fearless thoughts reveal;
And in her girdle was a skeyne of steel;
Her crimson mantle, a gold brooch did bind;
Her flowing garments reached unto her heel;
Her hair-part fell in tresses unconfined,
And part, a silver bodkin did fasten up behind.

'Twas not her garb that caught the gazer's eye -
Tho' strange, 'twas rich, and, after its fashion, good -
But the wild grandeur of her mien-erect and high.
Before the English Queen she dauntless stood,
And none her bearing there could scorn as rude;
She seemed as one well used to power -one that hath
Dominion over men of savage mood,
And dared the tempest in its midnight wrath,
And thro' opposing billows cleft her fearless path.

And courteous greeting Elizabeth then pays,
And bids her welcome to her English land
And humble hall. Each looked with curious gaze
Upon the other's face, and felt they stand
Before a spirit like their own. Her hand
The stranger raised -and pointing where all pale,
Thro' the high casement, came the sunlight bland,
Gilding the scene and group with rich avail;
Thus, to the English Sov'reign, spoke proud 'Grana Wale'.

Queen of the Saxons! From the distant west
I come; from Achill steep and Island Clare, .
Where the wild eagle builds 'mid clouds, his nest,
And Ocean flings its billows in the air. ",
I come to greet you in your dwelling fair.
Led by your fame -lone sitting in my cave.
In sea -beat Doona- it hath reached me there,
Theme of the minstrel's song; and then I gave
My galley to the wind, and crossed the dark green wave.

'Health to thee, ladye!' -let your answer be
Health to our Irish land; for evil men
Do vex her sorely, and have buklar'd thee
Abettor of their deeds; lyeing train,
That cheat their mistress for the love of gain,
And wrong their trust -aught else I little reck,
Alike to me, the mountain and the glen -
The castle's rampart or the galley's deck;
But thou my country spare -your foot is on her neck.

Thus brief and bold, outspake that ladye stem,
And all stood silent thro' that crowded hall;
While proudly glared each proud and manly kern
Attendant on their mistress. Then courtly all
Elizabeth replies, and soothing fall
Her words, and pleasing to the Irish ear –
Fair promises – that she would soon recall
Her evil servants. Were these words sincere?
That promise kept? Let Erin answer with a tear!

O'Hart: *Irish Pedigrees*, vol.II, p. 675

## Grana Weal

O thou that are sprung from the flow'r of the land,
Whose virtues endear and whose talents command;
When our foemen are banished, how then wilt thou feel
That the King of the right shall espouse Grana Weal.

O'er the high hills of Erin what bonfires shall blaze,
What libations be pour'd forth! – What festival days! –
What minstrels and monks with one heart-pulse of zeal,
Sing and pray for the King and his own Grana Weal!

The monarch of millions is riding the sea,
His revenge cannot sleep, and his guards will not flee;
No cloud shall the pride of our nobles conceal,
When the foes are dispersed that benight Grana Weal.

The mighty in thousands are pouring from Spain,
The Scots, the true Scots shall come back again;
To far-distant exile no more shall they steal,
But waft the right King to his fond Grana Weal.

Raise your hearts and exult, my beloved at my words,
Your eyes to your King, and your hand to your swords! –
The Highlands shall send forth the bonneted Gael,
To grace the glad nuptials of Grana Weal.

And Louis, and Charles and the heaven-guided Pope,
And the King of the Spaniards shall strengthen our hope;
One religion – one kindred – one soul shall they feel,
For our heart enthroned Exile and Grana Weal.

With weeping and wailing, and sorrow and shame –
And anguish of heart that no pity dare claim;
The craven English churls shall all powerless kneal
To the home-restored Stuart and Grana Weal.

Our halls will rejoice with friendship and cheer,
And our hearts be as free from reproach as from fear;
The hungry adventurer shall pine from the meal,
He long lapped from the life-stream of Grana Weal.
Ah! Knowest thou the maiden all beauteous and fair,
Whom her merciless foes have left plundered and bare?
The force of my emblem too well cant thou feel,
For that suffering lorn one is our Grana Weal.

But the nobles shall bring back the true king again
And justice long slighted will come in his train;
The bullets shall fly – and the cannons shall peal –
And our Charles victorious espouse Grana Weal.

James Hardiman: *Irish Minstrelsy*, vol. II, p. 65


### Grace O'Malley

She left the close-air'd, land of trees,
And proud MacWilliam's palace,
For clear, bare Clare's health-salted breeze,
Her oarsmen and her galleys
And where, beside the bending strand
The rock and billow wrestle
Between the deep sea and the land
She built her island Castle

The Spanish captain, sailing by
For Newport, with amazement
Beheld the cannon'd longship lie
Moor'd to the lady's casement,
And, covering coin and cup of gold
In haste their hatches under,
They whisper'd "Tis a pirate's hold;
She sails the seas for plunder.'

But no: 'twas not for sordid spoil
Of barque or sea-board borough
She plough'd, with unfatiguing toil,
The fluent – rolling furrow;
Delighting, on the broad back'd deep,
To feel the quivering galley
Strain up the opposing hill, and sweep
Down the withdrawing valley:

Or, sped before a driving blast,
By following seas uplifted,
Catch, from the huge heaps heaving past,
And from the spray they drifted
And from the winds that toss'd the crest
Of each wide-shouldering giant,
The smack of freedom and the zest
Of rapturous life defiant.

For, oh the mainland time was pent
In close constraint and striving,
So many aims together bent
On winning and on thriving;
There was no room for generous case,
No sympathy for candour: –
And so she left Burke's buzzing trees,
And all his stony splendour.

For Erin yet had fields to spare
Where Clew her cincture gathers
Isle – gemmed; and kindly clans were there,
The fosterers of her fathers:
Room there for careless feet to roam
Secure from minions' peeping
For fearless mirth to find a home
And sympathetic weeping;

And generous ire and frank disdain
To speak the mind, nor ponder
How this in England, that in Spain,
Might suit to tell; as yonder,
Where daily on the slippery dais
By thwarting interests chequer'd
State gamesters played the social chess
Of politic Clanrickard.

Nor wanting quite the lovely isle
In civic life's adornings:
The Brehon's Court, might well beguile
A learned lady's mornings.
Quaint through the clamorous claim, and rude
The pleading that convy'd it,
Right conscience made the judgment good,
And loyal love obey'd it.

And music was sweeter far
For ears of native nurture,
Than virginals at Castlebar
To tinkling touch of courtier,
Where harpers good in hall struck up
The planxty's gay commotion,
Or, pipers scream'd from pennon'd poop
Their piobrach over ocean.

And sweet, to see, their ruddy bloom
Whom ocean's friendly distance
Preserved still unenslaved; for whom
No tasking if existence
Made this one rich and that one poor,
In gold's illusive treasure,
But all, of easy life secure,
Were rich in wealth of leisure.

Rich in the Muse's pensive hour,
In genial hour for neighbour,
Rich in young mankind's happy power
To live with little labour;
The wise, free way of life, indeed,
That still, with charm adaptive,
Reclaims and tames the alien greed,
And takes the conqueror captive.

Nor only life's unclouded looks
To compensate its rudeness;
Amends there were in holy books,
In offices of goodness,
In cares above the transient scene
Of little gains and honours,
That well repaid the Island Queen
Her loss of urban manners.

Sweet, when crimson sunsets glow'd,
As earth and sky grow grander,
Adown the grass'd, unechoing road
Atlantic ward to wander,
Some Kinsman's humbler hearth to seek,
Some sick-bed side, it may be,
Or, onward reach, with footsteps meek,
The low, grey, lovely, abbey:

And, where stories stone beneath
The guise of plant and creature,
Had fused the harder lines of faith
In easy forms of nature;
Such forms, on tell the master's pains
'Mong Roslin's carven glories,
Or hint the faith of Pictish' Thanes
On standing stones of Forres;

The Branch; the weird cherubic Beasts;
The Hart by hounds o'ertaken;
Or, intimating mystic feasts,
The self-resorbent Dragon; –
Mute symbols, though with power endow'd
For finer dogmas' teaching,
Than clerk might tell to carnal crowd
In homily or preaching; –

Sit; and while heaven's refulgent show
Grew airier and more tender,
And ocean gleaming floor below
Reflected loftier splendour,
Suffused with light, of lingering faith
And ritual lights reflection,
Discourse of birth, and life, and death,
And of the resurrection.

But chiefly sweet from morn to eve,
From eve to clear-eyed morning,
The presence of the felt reprieve,
From strangers' note and scorning:
No prying, proud, intrusive foes
To pity and offend her: -
Such was the life the lady chose,
Such choosing, we commend her.

*Sir Samuel Ferguson.*

The following song originated in Co. Leitrim around Ballinamuck and
it is thought that it originated about 1798 with the survivors from Mayo of the
Battle at Ballinamuck between the Franco–Irish forces and the English.

### Granuaile

As the sunlight in its glory
Ever shines on fair Clew Bay
And Croagh Patrick old and hoary
Rises o'er the ruins grey
As the streamlets in the meadows
In their pride come dancing down
Nestled close among the mountains
Stands pleasant Newport Town.

Just a mile from where the turrets
Of the ancient town uprise
And the frowning peak of Nephin
Soars in grandeur to the skies
Lie a massive heap of ruins
In their loneliness sublime
Though scattered and dismantled now
By tyranny and time

'Twas a proud and stately castle
In the years of long ago
When the dauntless Grace O'Malley
Ruled a queen in fair Mayo.
And from Bernham's lofty summit ",
To the waves of Galway Bay
And from Castlebar to Ballintra
Her unconquered flag held sway.

She had strongholds on her headlands
And brave galleys on the sea
And no warlike chief or viking
E'er had bolder heart than she.
She unfurled her country's banner
High o'er battlement and mast
And 'gainst all the might of England
Kept it flying 'til the last.

The armies of Elizabeth
Invaded her on land
Her warships followed on her track
And watched by many a stand
But she swept her foes before her
On the land and on the sea
And the flag of Grace O'Malley
Waved defiant, proud and free.

On the walls of Carrick Clooney
As the Summer sun went down
And its last bright rays were fading
On the spires of Newport town.
To the watchmen on the ramparts
There appeared in long array
A band of English spearmen
By the waters of Clew Bay.

To the walls flew Grace O'Malley
With her clansmen at her side
Who had often met the foemen
On the land and on the tide.
But she saw the marshalled strength
Of the English coming on
And the colour of their armour
That in polished brightness shone.

Soon before the frowning battlements
The English columns came
Whilst on the walls before them
Stood many a bristling gun.
Then forwards towards the barbican
A herald quickly came
And demanded free admittance
In the English monarch's name.

He said 'My Royal Mistress
Sends her men-at-arms and me
With greetings good to all her friends
Who true and loyal be.
Her liegeman, Lord Hal Sydney
With all his spears awaits
For you to open wide to him
The Barbican and gates!

'So tell your Royal mistress,'
The dauntless Grace replied,
'That she and all her men-at-arms
Are scornfully defied.
She may own the fertile valley
Where the Foyle and Liffey flow
But tell her Grace O'Malley
Is unconquered in Mayo.'

'Our flag upon the battlements
Is to the breeze outthrown
And with God's grace we'll keep it there
In spite of Queen and throne.
There's many a brave O'Malley here
With me to man the walls
And rally round the flag we love
Until the last man falls!

'We want no English hirelings here
No soldiers of the Crown
We falter not before their spears
Nor cower beneath their frown.
No! Clansmen, let your warcry ring
Defiance on the gale
And greet those braggart Saxons
With a shower of Irish hail.'

Then sprang upon the Britons
With many a loud hurrah
A band of fierce and rugged men
Well brazed in many a fray.
On every tower and battlement "
The Irish kern appears
And fiercely flash their guns upon
The foe's advancing spears.

The dauntless Grace with Spartan soul
Stands on the outer wall.
Regardless of the shower of balls
That fast around them fall.
The English come with marshalled strength
And nerved with deadly hate
They fiercely clash through friends and foes
And gain the foremost gate.

But right before them face to face
The clansmen of Mayo
Start up and greet those robbers well
With thrust and sabre blow.
And rushing fierce as mountain stream
Through dark and flooded glen
Leaps to the gate, the dauntless Grace
And all her fearless men.

Hurrah! Their spears are backward borne
Their blood-red flag is down
And Sydney vanquished and pursued
Spurs hard to Newport Town.
This lesson taught the Saxon churl
To dread a Free-man's blow
When the dauntless Grace O'Malley
Ruled a Queen in fair Mayo.

The walls of Carrick Clooney
Now lie crumbling and low
Its battlements dismantled are
All moss o'er every stone.
But the rebel youth in Westport
Feel their Irish hearts aglow
When they tell how Grace O'Malley
Fought and conquered in Mayo.

There's many a fearless rebel
In Westport and Clew Bay
Who watch with longing eagerness
For Freedom's dawning day.
There's many a brawny mountaineer
Prepared to strike a blow
For the old Green Flag and Freedom
On the soil of brave Mayo.

*James Hardiman: Irish Minstrelsy, vol. II*

## Oró, Sé do Bheatha 'bhaile

### I

Sé do bheatha! a bhean ba leanmhar!
B'é ár gceach tú bheith i ngéibhinn,
Do dhuiche bhrea i seilbh meirleach
'S tú diolta leis na Gallaibh.

Oró! Sé do bheatha 'bhaile!
Oró! Sé do bheatha 'bhaile!
Oró! Sé do bheatha 'bhaile!
Anois ar theacht an tSamhraidh.

### II

Tá Gráinne Mhaol ag teacht thar sáile,
Óglaigh armtha leí mar gharda;
Gaeil iad féin 's ní Gaill ná Spainnigh
'S cuirfid ruaig ar Ghallaibh

### III

A bhuí le Rí na bhfeart go bhfeiceam,
Muna mbeam beo 'na dhiaidh ach seachtain,
Gráinne Mhaol agus míle gaiscíoch
Ag fógairt fáin ar Ghallaibh.

*Pádraig Mac Phiarais*

## Oró and Welcome Home

### I

Welcome, O woman who was sorrowful
We were desolate while you were imprisoned.
Your lovely country in the hands of vandals
And you yourself – sold to the English.

Chorus:
Oró – and welcome home,
Oró – and welcome home,
Oró – and welcome home,
Would that the Summer is here.

### II

Gráinne Mhaol is coming over the sea,
With a guard of young soldiers,
They are Irish, not English or Spanish
And they will rout the English.

### III

Thanks be to God that I'm seeing
(Even If I only live for a week after!)
Gráinne Mhaol and a thousand warriors
Announcing ruin on the English.

*Pádraig Pearse (translated)*

### Granuweal – An old song

A courtier call'd Dorset, from Parkgate did fail,
In his Majesty's yacht, for to court Granuweal;
With great entertainment the thought to prevail,
And rifle the charms of Granuweal.

Chorus:
Sing Budderoo, didderoo, Granuweal,
The Fox in the Trap we have caught by the tail
Sing success to the sons of brave Granuweal.

### II

Says the courtier to Granu, if you will be true,
I will bring you to London, and do for you too;
Where you shall have pleasure that never will fail,
I'll laurel your Shamrock, sweet Granuweal.

### III

Says Granu to Dorset, if that I would do,
Bring my fortune to London, my children would rue;
We would be like Highlanders eating of keal,
And cursing the union, says Granuweal.

### IV

Says Granu, I always was true to my king;
When in war, I supply'd him with money and men.
Our love to King George with our blood we did seal,
At Dettingen battle, says Granuweal.

### V

Says Granu, I always still lov'd to be free;
No foe shall invade me in my liberty.
While I've Limerick, Derry and the fort of Kinsale,
I'll love and not marry, says Granuweal.

### VI

Says Granu, you see there's a large stone put in,
To the heart of the church, by the leave of the King.
The works of this stone shall be weigh'd in a scale,
With balance of justice, says Granuweal.

### VII

I hope our brave Harrington, likewise Kildare,
Our trade and our commerce once more will repair,
Our lives we will venture with greatest affail,
Against French and Spaniards, says Granuweal.

### VIII

Now, my dear boys, we've got shut of those bugs,
I charge you my children, lie close in your rugs,
They'll hide like a snake, but will bite I'll be bail,
I'll give them shillelagh, says Granuweal.


## Poor Old Granuaile

My dream to some with joy will come and comes with grief to more,
As it did to me, my country, that dear old Erin's shore;
I dreamt I stood upon a hill beside a lovely vale,
And it's there I spied a comely maid and her name was Granuaile.

Her lovely hair hung down so fair and she was dressed in green,
I thought she was the fairest soul that e'er my eyes had seen;
As I drew near I then could hear by the pleasant morning gale,
As she went along she sang her song saying 'I'm poor old Granuaile'.

In O'Connell's time in '29 we had no braver men,
They struggled hard both day and night to gain our rights again;
Still, by coercion we were bound and our sons were sent to jail,
'You need not fret, we'll Home Rule get,' says poor old Granuaile.
I thought she had a splendid harp by her side she let it fall,
She played the tunes called Brian Boru, Garryowen, and Tara's Hall.
Then God Save Ireland was the next, and Our Martyrs Who Died in Jail,
'You need not fret, we'll have freedom yet,' says poor old Granuaile.

When I wakened from my slumber and excited by my fight,
I thought it was the clear daylight, and I found that it was night;
I looked all round and could see naught but the walls of a lonely jail.
And that was the last I ever saw of poor old Granuaile.

*Irish Street Ballads collected and annotated by*
*Colm Ó Loughlainn, London 1928*

### A New Song Called Granuaile

All through the north as I walked forth to view the shamrock plain
I stood a while where nature smiled amid the rocks and streams
On a matron mild I fixed my eyes beneath a fertile vale
As she sang her song it was on the wrongs of poor old Granuaile

Her head was bare and her grey hair over her eyes hung down
Her waist and neck, her hands and feet, with iron chains were bound
Her pensive strain and plaintive wail mingled with the evening gale
And the song she sung with mournful tongue was Poor Old Granuaile.

The gown she wore was stained with gore all by a ruffian band
Her lips so sweet that monarchs kissed are now grown pale and wan
The tears of grief fell from her eyes each tear as large as hail
None could express the deep distress of poor old Granuaile.

On her harp she leaned and thus exclaimed 'My royal Brian is gone
Who in his day did drive away the tyrants every one
On Clontarf's plains against the Danes his faction did prepare.
Brave Brian Boru cut their lines in two and freed old Granuaile.

'But now, alas, I must confess, avengers I have none
There's no brave Lord to wave his sword in my defence — not one
My enemies just when they please with blows they do assail
The flesh they tore clean off the bones of poor old Granuaile.

Six hundred years the briny tears have flowed down from my eyes
I curse the day that Henry made of me proud Albion's prize
From that day down with chains I'm bound no wonder I look pale
The blood they drained from every vein of poor old Granuaile.'

There was a lord came from the south he wore a laurel crown
Saying 'Grania dear, be of good cheer, no longer you'll be bound
I am the man they call great Dan, who never yet did fail
I have got the bill for to fulfil your wishes Granuaile.'

With blood besmeared and bathed in tears her harp she sweetly strung
And oh the change, her mournful air from one last chord she wrung
Her voice so clear fell on my ear, at length my strength did fail
I went away and thus did say, 'God help you, Granuaile'.

# *Granuaile's Family Tree*

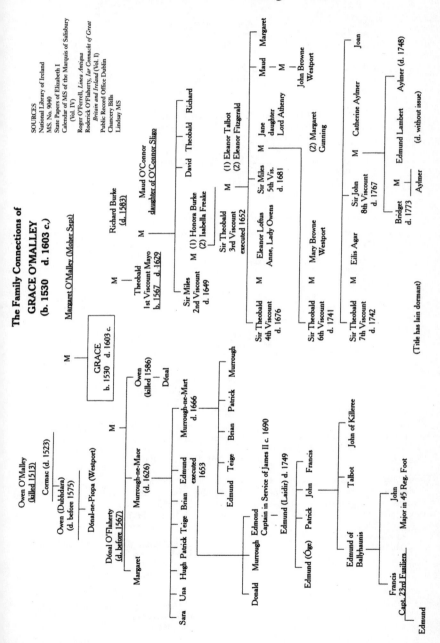

The Family Connections of
**GRACE O'MALLEY**
(b. 1530   d. 1603 c.)

SOURCES
National Library of Ireland
MS. No. 9040
State Papers of Elizabeth I
Calendar of MS of the Marquis of Salisbury
(Vol. IV)
Roger O'Ferrell, *Linea Antiqua*
Roderick O'Flaherty, *Iar Connacht or Great
Briain and Ireland* (Vol. I)
Public Record Office Dublin
Chancery Bills
Lindsay MS

# Descendants of Maud Bourke and John Browne

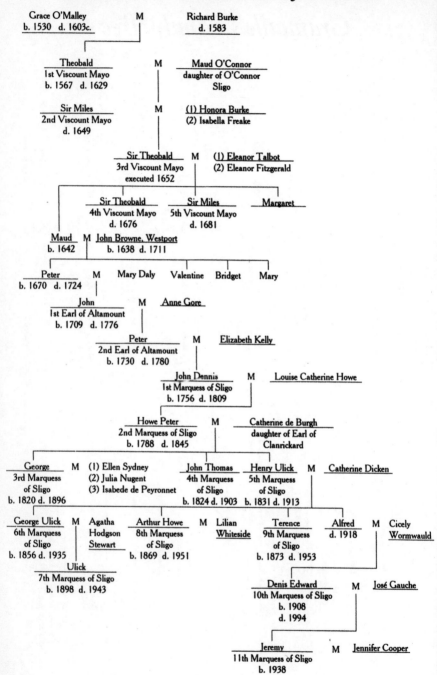

# Granuaile's Petition to Queen Elizabeth I, July 1593

## To the Queen's Most Excellent Majesty

In most humble Wise showeth unto your most excellent Majestie your loyall and faithful subject Grany ny Mally of Conaght in your highnes realm if Ireland:- that wheras by meanes of the continnuall discord stirres and dissention that heretofore long tyme remained among the Irishrye especially in West Conaght by the sea side every cheeftaine for his safegard and maintenance and for the defence of his people followers and countrye took armes by strong hand to make head against his neyborhes which in like manner constrained your highnes fond subject to take armes and by force to maintain her selfe and her people by sea and land the space of fortye yeares past. During which tyme she married Offlahertye being natural mother of his lawfull sone and heire nowe living and after his death married Mac William the cheefe of the Bourkes of West Conaght who died X yeares past, since which tyme she remaineth widowe and is likewise the mother of his lawfull sone and heyre nowe living. The countryes and teritories of which chieftaines after the rude custome of their ancestores never yeilded doweries or thirds to the ladies thereof, and the rents services and reservation of the same was not certayne but confused the people for yelding to the cheeftains whatever they would crave more than of ryght they aught to have. And now whereas by your gracious meanes the said province is reduced to that civil course that the cheeftaines freeholders or gents. hath compounded and is assigned what and how much he is to have; in which composition no order was taken for your fond subject what maintenance she aught to have of her former husbands lands and by the same is restrayned to use her former course to her utter decay and ruine: In tender consideracon whereof and in regard of her great age she most humbly besechethe your Majestie if your princely bounty and liberaltye to grant her some reasonable maintenance for the little tyme she hath to lyve. And whereas your said subjects two sones are the lawfull heyres of the lands of there foresaid fathers whereof they nowe stand seized and possessed, that it would please your Royall Majestie to direct your gracious letters to your L. Deputy of your said realme willing him to accept a surrender at her hands of her said sones yelding to Your Majestie your heyrs and successors such yearly rents as conventiently such lands may yeld and they to hold the same by letters patents to them and ther heyres for ever and to grant the like for the lands of Walter Burgh Fitz Theobald Reogh and Shane Burke Mac William Mac Moiler cosen germaine to her said son. And lastly that it would please your Majestie to grant unto your said subject under your most gracious hand of signet free libertye during her lyve to envade with sword and fire all your highnes enemyes whersoever they ar or shal be without any interruption of any person or persons whatsoever. Thus shall your said subject according to her bounden duty ever remayne in all obedient alleagance to resist all remnants of rebellious enemies and pray continually for your Majesties long life and prosperous reygne.

*Source:* State Papers Elizabeth I.

Deciphered from the original by author.

# Petition of Grany ny Mally to the Lord Treasurer, 5 May 1595

To the right honorable and my very good lord high treasurer of England.

Right Honorable and my very good lo. maye it hath pleased her Matie. At my last beinge here by her highness letters to Sr Richard Bingham to demand hime to take present order that I might possess and injoie the third parte of the lands and comodities of Mac William and O'Flahertie as lawful wif unto each of them so it is right honorable that I cane not have nor can injoie the same by meenes of Sir Richard Binghams hard dealing. I therefore most humblie beseeche your honours to be a meynes to her Matie to addres mye her highnes letters to the lo. Deputie to put me in the possession of the third parte of the said Mac William and O'Flahertie my late husbands land and lyvinge and that likewise I may lyve secure of my life which hath been atempted sundrie tymes to be said Sr Richard Bingham his brethern and others by his direcsion, humbly I beg your Treas.'s favourable letters in my owne and me sonnes behalf to the lo Deputie and to Sr Richard Bingham so cravinge pardon for my contynuall boldness … the living God to blesse and preserve yor Lord.

*Source:* State Papers Elizabeth I.

Deciphered from the original by author.

# Signed Letter by Theobald Bourke – Tibóid-ne-Long (Toby of the Ships), to Anthony Brabazon, English Commissioner to Connaught

I have received your Honors letters and according as I have formerly written that I should be advertised of the meeting doiet eight daies before the appointeing thereof: I have not received the said advertisement but the eight of this month wheras you would have me to meete the IX of this month. Wherefore I desire yor. Honor to forbeare till the eighteen of this month and in the meane time, we will prepare our complaints and agrevances and will be provided with provisions and other necessaries wch cannot be done before that time. As for Odonelle I perceive by his letters that he is likewise to answeare in that case for others in Connought and do here he will be ther the daie before menconed. Further for as much as Gallaway men do not furnishe us with anie commodities wee desire yor. Honor to direct yor. warrant unto the Mayor to th'end that we maye be furnished with such things as ys expedient excepting munitions of warres and with all to send a provision for those as will repaire for things to Gallawaye. Thus desiring yor. Honor to do not faile therin. I bide yo hartely farewell. Ffrom camp the VIIIth of June 1596.

Signed Theobald Bourk

*Source:* State Papers Elizabeth I.

Deciphered from the original by author.

# The Eighteen
## 'Articles of Interrogatory'

## TO BE ANSWERED BY GRANY NIMALY

1. Who was her father and mother?
2. Who was her first husband?
3. What sons she had by him? What be their names and where they live?
4. What countries they have to maintain them withal?
5. To whom they be married?
6. What kin was O'Flaherty her first husband to Sir Mourrough Ne Dough O'Flaherty that is here now at the court?
7. To answer the like question for her 2 husband and for his sons and their livings.
8. If she were to be allowed her dower, or thirds of her husbands living of what value the same might be of?
9. Where upon the Composition of Connaught there hath been any provisions for the wives?
10. Whether it be not against the Customs of Ireland for the wives to have more after the deaths of their husbands than they brought with them?
11. How she hath had maintenance and living since her last husband's death?
12. Of what kindred is Walter Bourgh fitz Tibalds and Shane Bourke mc Moyler to her son?
13. What captains and countries lie next to her husband's possessions?
14. Who doth possess the house of Moriske upon the seaside in Owle O'Maly?
15. What lands doth McGibbon possess in that country?
16. Who doth possess the country named Carramore and Mayn Connell?
17. Who doth possess the island of Achill and Kill castle?
18. What kin was her last husband to Walter and Ulick Bourke?

## ANSWERS OF GRANY NY MALLY TO THE ARTICLES

*To the first*
Her father was called Doodarro O Mailly sometime chieftain of the
country called Opper Owle O Mailly now called the barony of
Murasky her mother was called Margaret ny Mailly daughter to
Conogher Omailly of the same country and family. The whole
country of Owle O Mailly aforesaid have these islands viz. Inish
Bofyne Cleria Inish Twirke Inish arke Caher Inishdalluff Davellen
and other small islands of little value which and the rest of the
mainland are divided into the towns to the number of twenty and
to every town four quarter or ploughs of land is assigned; out of
every such quarter of land is yearly paid to her Majesty ten shillings
called the composition rent. There is also in Connaught a country
called Owle Eighter, otherwise the Lower or Nether Owle,
containing fifty towns at four quarters the town, yearly paying the
same rent, whereof the Sept of the Mailles in general hath twenty
towns, the Bourkes of Mac William country other twenty towns
and the Earl of Ormond ten towns.

*To the second*
Her first husband was called Donell Ichoggy Offlaherty and during
his life chieftain of the Barony of Ballynehenssy, containing
twenty-four towns at four quarters of land to every town paying
yearly the composition rent aforesaid. After his death Teige
Offlaherty the eldest son of Sir Morough now at court entered into
Ballynehenssy afore said there did build a strong castle and the
same with the demain lands thereof kept many years. Which Teige
in the last rebellion of his father was slain.

*To the third*
She had two sons by her said first husband the eldest called Owen
Offlahertie married Katherine Bourke daughter of Edmond
Bourke of Castle Barry by her he had a son named Donell
Offlahertie, now living which Owen all his lifetime remained a true
subject to Her Majesty under the government of Sir Nicholas
Malby while he lived and under Sir Richard Bingham until July
1586 at which time the Bourkes of the McWilliams country and the

sept of the Shoose [Joyce] began to rebel.  The said Owen, according to Sir Richards special direction, did withdraw himself his followers and tenants, with all their goods and cattle into a strong island for their more and better assurance.  Then having been sent against the said rebels five hundred soldiers under the leading of Captain John Bingham appointed by his brother Sir Richard Bingham as the lieutenant in those parts.  When they missed both the rebels and their cattle they came to the mainland right against the said island calling for victualls; whereupon the said Owen came forth with a number of boats and ferried all the soldiers into the island where they were entertained with the best cheer they had.  That night the said Owen was apprehended and tied with a rope with eighteen of his chief followers; in the morning the soldiers drew out of the island four thousand cows, five hundred stud mares and horses and a thousand sheep leaving the remainder of the poor men all naked within the island [they] came with the cattle and prisoners to Ballynehenssy afor said where John Bingham afor said stayed for their coming; that evening he caused the said eighteen persons without trial or good cause to be hanged among whom was hanged a gentleman of land and living called Thebault O Twohill being of the age of four score and ten years. The next night following a false alarm was raised in the camp in the dead of the night the said Owen was cruelly murdered having twelve deadly wounds and in that miserable sort he ended his years and unfortunate days – Captain William Mostyn now at court and Captain Merriman and Captain Mordant were of that company. Her second son called Moroghe Offlahertie now living is married to Honora Bourke daughter to Richard Bourke of Derivillaghny in the Magheri Reagh within the county of Galway.

*To the fourth*
Moroghe her second son aforesaid and Donell son to her first son the aforesaid Owen murdered do possess and enjoy the fourth part of Barony of Ballynehenssy aforesaid unto them descended from their ancestors which is all the maintenance they have.

*To the fifth*
This is answered more at large to the third article.

*To the sixth*
Her first husband by the mother's side of Sir Moroghe now at court was his cousin germain and also cousins both being descended of one stock and root of nine degrees of consanguinity asunder.

*To the seventh*
Her second husband was called Sir Richard Bourke Knight alias McWilliam chief of the Bourkes of Nether or Low Connaught by him she had a son called Theobald Bourke now living he is married to Mewffe O'Connor sister to O'Connor Sligo now at court, his inheritance is about 40 quarters of land situated in the three baronies of Carry [Carra], Nether Owel and Galling [Gallen].

*To the eight*
The countries of Connaught among the Irishry never yielded any thirds to any woman surviving the chieftain whose rent was uncertain for the most part extorted but now made certain by the composition and all Irish exactions merely abolished.

*To the ninth*
The Composition provided nothing to relieve the wife of any chieftain after his death wherein no mention is made of any such.

*To the tenth*
Among the Irishry the custom is that wives shall have but her first dowry without any increase or allowance for the same time out of mind it hath been so used and before any woman do deliver up her marriage portion to her husband she receives sureties for the restitution of the same in manner and form as she hath delivered it in regard that husbands through their great expenses especially chieftains at the time of their deaths have no goods to leave behind them but are commonly indebted; at other times they are divorced upon proof of precontracts; and the husband now and then without any lawful or due proceeding do put his wife from him and so bringeth in another; so as the wife is to have sureties for her dowry for fear of the worse.

*To the eleventh*
After the death of her last husband she gathered together all her

own followers and with 1,000 head of cows and mares departed and became a dweller in Carrikahowlly in Borisowle parcel of the Earl of Ormond's lands in Connaught and in the year 1586 after the murdering of her son Owen the rebellion being then in Connaught Sir Richard Bingham granted her his letters of tuition against all men and wiled her to remove from her late dwelling at Borisowle and to come and dwell under him, in her journey as she travelled was encountered by the five bands of soldiers under the leading of John Bingham and thereupon she was apprehended and tied in a rope, both she and her followers at that instant were spoiled of their said cattle and of all that ever they had besides the same and brought to Sir Richard who caused a new pair of gallows to be made for her last funeral where she thought to end her days, she was let at liberty upon the hostage and pledge of one Richard Bourke otherwise called the Devil's Hook when he did rebel fear compelled her to fly by sea into Ulster and there with O'Neill and O'Donnell staid three months; her galleys by a tempest being broken. She returned to Connaught and in Dublin received her Majesty's pardon by Sir John Perrot six years past and so made free. Ever since she dwelleth in Connaught a farmers life very poor bearing cess and paying Her Majesty's composition rent, utterly did she give over her former trade of maintenance by sea and land.

### To the twelfth

Walter Bourke FitzThebalt and Shane Bourke FitzMeiller are cousins germain removed of one side viz. Walter son to Thebault, son to Meiller so to the said Walter Faddy. Thebault Bourke mentioned in the seventh article and borne by Grany Ny Mailly son to Sir Richard Bourke her last husband, which Sir Richard was brother to the said Walter Faddy.

### To the thirteenth

The country of her first husband is situated between Owle O'Mailley on the north west part, Mac William's country to the north east towards the country of Sligo, Sir Moroghe Offlaherties country on the east side towards Galway and the great bay of Galway on the south.

*To the fourteenth*
The castle town and lands of Morrisky is possessed by Owen M'Thomas O'Mailley now chieftain by the name of O'Mailley.

*To the fifteenth*
The Mac Gibbons have no lands by inheritance in any part of the country; farmers they are at will both to the Bourkes and to the O'Maillies.

*To the sixteenth*
She doth not know or understand Caremore or Moinconnell.

*To the seventeenth*
The island of Ackill is occupied by some of the Mailleys as tenants to the Earl of Ormond, as for Kill Castle, she knoweth no town of that name.

*To the eighteenth*
Her last husband had two brothers Walter and Ulligge [Ulick] Bourke both died before she married Sir Richard Bourke, her said husband, their father was called David Bourke.

A set of 18 questions by Lord Burghley, the Lord Treasurer of England, dated July 1593 with answers by Granuaile.

*Source:* State Papers, Elizabeth I.

Deciphered from the original by the author.

# References

**Ch. 1: Powerful by Land and Sea**
1. MS 1440, TCD.
2. Ordnance Survey Letters, Mayo, vol. II, p.97.
3. *The Stranger in Ireland*, p.304.
4. *A Chorographical Description of West Connaught*, p.140.
5. *Ibid.*
6. *History of the County Mayo*, p.189.
7. *Revue Celtique*, vol. XLIX, p.174.
8. *Annals of the Four Masters*, vol. II, p.1019.
9. *Ibid.* vol. 4, p.815.
10. *Revue Celtique*, vol. XLIX, p.175.
11. *History of the Town and County of Galway*, p.83.
12. *Ibid.* p.64.
13. *Ibid.* p.201.
14. *Annals of Ulster*, vol. 3, p.69.
15. SPI 63/19/56.
16. *Bold in Her Breeches*, p.21.
17. Calendar of State Papers (Elizabeth I), vol. CCV, p.335.
18. *Ibid.* vol. CCVl, p.335.
19. Lord of the Isles Voyage Brochure.
20. Calendar State Papers (Elizabeth I), vol. CCVl, p.89.
21. Calendar of State Papers (Elizabeth I), vol. CCVl, p.335;

**Ch. 2: The World of Granuaile**
1. Ordnance Survey Letters, Mayo, vol. II.
2. The Discourses, Book III, ch.26.
3. Discourse of Ireland, p.357.
4. Chancery Bill, no. R.63.
5. Calendar State Papers (Edward VI), vol. CLXX, p.132.
6. *Beginnings of Modern Ireland*, p.30.
7. *A Chorographical Description of West Connaught*, p.58.
8. Royal Irish Academy, MS no AV2, Folio 53A.
9. *The Buccaneer Queen*, p.24.
10. *Irish Life in the 17th Century*, p.338.
11. *Social History of Ancient Ireland*, p.284.
12. *Ibid.*
13. *A Chorographical Description of West Connaught*, p.383.

**Ch. 3: Fortuna Favet Fortibus**
1. *Irish Life in the 17th Century*, p.338.
2. Ordnance Survey Letters, Mayo, vol.II, p.97.
3. SPI 63/170/63.
4. *Ibid.*
5. Calendar State Papers (Elizabeth 1), vol. CCVII, p.5.
6. Dept. Celtic Studies, ms. no.532.
7. *A Chorographical Description of West Connaught*, p. 385.
8. SPI 63/170/63.
9. *Ibid.*
10. SPI 63/170/19.

**Ch. 4: The Pirate Queen**
1 SPI 63/170/204.
2 SPI 63/171/18.
3 Lambeth Palace Library, ms. no.601, p.111.
4 Calendar State Papers (James 1) 1623, no.997.
5 Ordnance Survey Letters, Mayo, vol. II.
6 Dept Celtic Studies, Folklore Collection, ms. no.1134.
7 *The Way That I Went*, p. 184.
8 *Great Book of Genealogies*, p.3259.
9 Gaisford St Lawrence Papers.
10 *Howth and its Owners*, p182.
11 Ordnance Survey Letters, Mayo, vol. II.

**Ch. 5: 'A Most Famous Feminine Sea Captain'**

1 Calendar State Papers (Elizabeth 1), vol. 72, no.39.
2 *Gaelic and Gaelicised Ireland,* p 73.
3 Lambeth Palace Library, ms. no.601, p.111.
4 *Ibid.*
5 SPI 63/170/63.
6 *Hibernia Dominicana,* p.319.
7 Ordnance Survey Letters, Mayo, vol. I. p.l.
8 Royal Irish Academy, ms. no. Av2 Folio 53A.
9 *Filí agus Filídheacht Chonnacht,* p.267.
10 *Gaelic and Gaelicised Ireland,* p.79.
11 *History of the County Mayo,* p.181.
12 Calendar Carew MSS, vol. II, p.38.
13 *Ulster Journal of Archaeology,* vol.V, p.299.
14 Lambeth Palace Library, ms. no. 601, p.101.
15 *Ibid .*
16 SPI 63/19/56.
17 *Ibid.*
18 *Ibid.*
19 SPI 63/19/78.
20 *History of the Town and County of Galway,* p.86.
21 *The Geraldines,* p.279.
22 *As Wicked A Woman,* p.133.
23 Calendar of State Papers (Elizabeth I), vol. CXX, no.39.
24 *Ibid.*
25 Calendar of Carew MSS, vol. 11, no.322.
26 SPI 63/172/63.
27 *Ibid.*
28 *Chieftain to Knight,* p.43.
29 Westport House MSS.
30 *Ibid.*
31 *Ibid.*

**Chapter 6:**
**'Nurse to all Rebellions'**

1 Calendar State Papers (Elizabeth I), vol. CLXX, p.132.
2 Ordnance Survey Letters, Mayo vol. II.
3 *Ibid.*
4 Westport House MSS.
5 *Ibid.*
6 Analecta Hibernia, p.133.
7 Calendar State Papers (Elizabeth I), vol. XCIX, p. 424.
8 *Ibid.*
9 *Ibid.*
10 *Annals of the Four Masters,* vol. V, p.1805.
11 *Ibid.*
12 SPI 63/170/63.
13 *Annals of Loch Cé,* vol.II, p. 459.
14 Westport House MSS.
15 *Ibid.*
16 *Anecdotes and Traditions,* p.18.
17 Calendar State Papers (Elizabeth I), vol. CLXX, p.128.
18 *Political Works of Edmund Spenser,* p.67.
19 Royal Irish Academy, ms. no. AV1, Folio 53A.
20 Titus BXIII, p. 410.
21 MSS Marquis of Salisbury, vol. III, p. 285.
22 SPI 63/170/63.
23 Titus BXIII, p.236.
24 SPI 63/158/37.
25 SPI 63/170/63.
26 *Ibid.*
28 SPI 63/158/37.
29 *Ibid.*
30 Elizabethan Epic, p.182.
31 SPI 63/170/63.
32 Calendar of Fiants (Elizabeth I), no.5173.
33 SPI 63/170/63.

**Chapter 7:**
**'A Notable Traitoress'**

1 Westport House MSS.
2 *Ibid.*
3 SPI 63/145/6.
4 Calendar State Papers (Elizabeth I), vol. CLXV, no.6.

5 Titus BX111, p.446.
6 SPI 63/147/35.
7 SPI 63/146/35.
8 Calendar State Papers (Elizabeth I), vol. CLXVII, no.13.
9 *Ibid.* no.81.
10 SPI 63/171/18.
11 *Ibid.*
12 SPI 63/158/62.
13 *The Celtic Peoples and Renaissance Europe,* p.42.
14 Calendar State Papers (Elizabeth I), vol. CLXXI, p.141.
15 SPI 63/206/92.
16 *History of the County Mayo,* p.250.
17 *Ibid.*
18 *Irish Pedigrees,* vol. II, p. 675.

**Chapter 8:**
**The Meeting of the Two Queens**
1 SPI 63/170/204.
2 *Ibid.*
3 SPI 63/171/62.
4 63/170/44.
5 Dept Celtic Studies, Folklore, Schools MSS no.4, p.512.
6 SPI 63/171/37.
7 SPI 63/172/341.
8 *The Elizabethan Epic,* p. 74.
9 SPI 63/171/44.
10 SPI 63/170/63.
11 Calendar State Papers (Elizabeth I), vol. CLXX, p.132.
12 *Ibid.*
13 SPI 63/171/62.
14 The Elizabethan Epic, p.203.
15 *Ibid* p.73.
16 *Ibid* p. 142.
17 *Irish Pedigrees,* vol. II p.675.
18 *The Elizabethan Epic,* p.71.
19 Hatfield House, MSS Marquis of Salisbury, no. CP 169/128.
20 SPI 63/171/44.
21 Hatfield House, no. CP 169/128.
22 SPI 63/170/204.
23 Hatfield House, no. CP 169/128.
24 *Ibid.*
25 SPI 63/171/62.

26 *Ibid.*
27 *Ibid.*
28 SPI 63/171/44.
29 Hatfield House, no. CP 169/128.
30 *Ibid.*

**Chapter 9:**
**The End of an Era**
1 SPI 63/172/26.
2 *Ibid.*
3 SPI 63/179/81.
4 Calendar State Papers (Elizabeth I), vol. CCV1, no.92.
5 SPI 63/179/36.
6 *Ibid.*
7 *Ibid.*
8 SPI 63/179/35.
9 *Ibid.*
10 SPI 63/179/70.
11 *Ibid.*
12 *Ibid.*
13 *Ibid.*
14 Calendar of Fiants, Elizabeth, no.5948.
15 *History of Ireland,* vol III, p.122.
16 Calendar State Papers (Elizabeth I), 1592-96, preface XXVI.
17 *Life of Hugh Roe O'Donnell,* p.111.
18 *Scots Mercenary Forces in Ireland,* p.142.
19 *Annals of the Four Masters,* vol. IV, p. 2013.
20 *Ibid* .
21 Calendar State Papers (Elizabeth I), vol. CC, p.376.
22 *Ibid.* vol. CCVIII, p. 436.
23 SPI 63/237/12

**Chapter 10:**
**The Descendants of Granuaile**
1 *Chieftain to Knight,* p. 11.
2 Calendar of Carew MSS, vol. III, p.490.
3 *Ibid.* vol. VIII, p. 136.
4 Galway Archaeological and Historical Society, vol.11, p.54.
5 *Funeral Entries Books,* vol.V, p.147.
6 Lindsay MS, PRO. of Dublin

# Bibliography

## 1. Manuscript Sources

British Library
Cotton Titus BX111, XV111, Papers on Irish affairs, 1559-1602,

Department of Celtic Studies, UCD
MSS nos. 86, 202, A229, 693, 838, 1134, 1181, 1206, 1238, 1838, 4844

Howth Castle, Co Dublin
Gaisford St. Lawrence papers

Genealogical Office, Dublin
MSS. nos 482-5, 699, 165, 155,
Funeral Entries Books, vol 2

Hatfield House, Hertfordshire
Cecil Papers no. 169/128

Lambeth Palace Library
MSS 601, 619

National Library of Ireland
State Papers relating to Ireland (on microfilm, originals in the Public
Record Office, London)
SP 63/19/56, 186, 63/61/74, 63/72/63, 63/88/34, 63/96/37,
63/145/6, 164, 63/146/35, 43I, 43II, 43III, 431V, 148, 63/147/18III,
63/158/37, 62, 63/170/44, 168, 204, 63/171/18, 37, 44, 62, 65, 81;
63/172/26, 34I, 63/173/1, 63, 63/179/35, 36, 36I, 38,70, 75, 77, 62-66,
63/199/66V, 66VI, 63/200/356, 63/206/20, 63/237/12.

Public Record Office, Ireland
Chancery Bills nos 1.209, R.63, R.65, A.A.150
Lindsay MS no. 6

Royal Irish Academy, Dublin
MSS nos. AV2 f.53A,

Westport House Manuscript Collection, Westport House, Co Mayo
(now in the National Library of Ireland).

## 2. Contemporary Sources
*Analecta Hibernia* nos, 8, 24, 26
*Annala Rioghachta Eireann. Annals of the Kingdom of Ireland by the Four
    Masters,* from the ealiest period to the year 1616, ed. and trans. J.
    O'Donovan. 7 vols, (Dublin 1851)
*Annals of Loch Cé. A Chronicle of Irish Affairs,* 1014-1590, ed. W.M.

Hennessy, 2 vols (London 1871).

*Annals of Ulster,* ed. B. MacCarthy, (Dublin 1893)

*Books of Survey and Distribution,* Mayo 1636-1703 (Dublin 1956)

Camden, W., *Britania* (London 1695)

Davis, Sir John, *A Discovery of the True Causes Why Ireland Was Never Entirely Subdued...* (London 1612), Facsimile reprint (Shannon 1969).

Derricke, J., *The Image of Ireland* (London 1581), Facsimile reprint (Belfast 1985)

Hogan, E. ed. *Description of Ireland* (Dublin 1878)

Hogan, E. and N. MacNeill, eds., *The Walsingham Letterbook,* May 1576 to December 1579 (Dublin 1959)

Holinshed, R., *Chronicles of England, Scotland and Ireland,* ed J. Johnson, (London 1807-8)

Moryson, F. *An Itinerary* (London 1617), Facsimile edition (Glasgow 1907-8)

*Sidney State Papers,* 1565-1570 ed. T O'Laidhin (Dublin) 1962.

O'Cleary, L., *The Life of Hugh Roe O'Donnell, Prince of Tirconail, 1586-1602* (Dublin 1893)

O'Donovan, J. ed and trans. *Leabhar na gCeart.* (The Book of Rights) (Dublin 1847)

O'Flaherty, R. *A Chorographical Description of West Connaught 1684,* (Dublin 1846)

Perrot, J., *The Chronicle of Ireland 1584-1608,* ed. H. Wood (Dublin 1933)

Spenser, E., *A View of the Present State of Ireland...* in 1596, ed W.l. Renwick (Oxford 1970)

Stafford, T., *Pacata Hibernia* (London 1633), ed. S. H. O'Grady (London 1896)

## Calendars and Printed Manuscript Sources

Calendar of the Carew Manuscripts, ed J.S Brewer and W. Bullen, 6 vols (London 1867-73).

Calendar of Cecil Manuscripts, 8 vols (London 1883-1899)

Calendar of Fiants of the Reign of Elizabeth, (Dublin 1877-94).

Calendar of Patent and Close Rolls of Chancery, Elizabeth ed., J. C. Morrin (Dublin 1862).

Calendar of the Manuscripts of the Marquis of Salisbury, (London 1883-1973)

Calendar of State Papers Relating to Ireland, (London 1860-1912).

Compossicion Booke of Connaught, ed. A Freeman (Dublin 1936)

Sidney State Papers, 1565-70, ed. T. O Laidhin (Dublin 1962).

Sidney, Letters and Memorials of State, written and collected by Sir Henry Sidney, Sir Philip Sidney and his brother, Sir Robert Sidney, ed. A. Collins (London 1746)

**Secondary Sources**

*Anthologia Hibernica*, vol.11 (Dublin 1793)

Bagwell, R., *Ireland under the Tudors*, 3 vols (London 1885-90)

Bagwell, R., *Ireland under the Stuarts*, 3 vols (London 1909-16)

Ball, F., *Howth and its Owners*, (Dublin 1917)

Beckett, J.C. *The Making of Modern Ireland* (London 1966)

Black, Clinton, *Pirates of the West Indies* (Cambridge Press 1989)

Black, J.B., *The Reign of Elizabeth, 1558-1603* (Oxford 1959

Blackwell, M., *Ships in Early Irish History* (Co. Clare 1992)

Butler, W.F.T. *Confiscation in Irish History* (1917)

Byrne, M., *Ireland Under Elizabeth* (Dublin 1903)

Callwell, J., *Old Irish Life* (London 1912)

Canny, N., *The Elizabethan Conquest. A Pattern Established, 1565-76* (1976)

Chambers, A., *Chieftain to Knight. Tibbott-ne-Long Bourke, Viscount Mayo, 1567-1629* (Dublin 1983)

Chambers, A., *As Wicked A Woman, Eleanor Countess of Desmond, 1545-1638* (Dublin 1989)

Cordingly, D., *Life Among the Pirates* (UK 1995)

Corkery, D., *The Hidden Ireland* (Dublin 1979)

Dutton, R., *English Court Life* (London 1963)

Ellis, S.G., *Tudor Ireland* (London 1985)

Fallon, N., *The Armada in Ireland* (London 1978)

Falls, C., *Elizabeth's Irish Wars* (London 1950)

FitzGerald, B., *The Geraldines, 1169-1601* (London 1951)

Hardiman, J., *History of the Town and County of Galway* (Dublin 1920)

Hardiman, J., *Irish Minstrelsy*, vol. II (London, 1831)

Ireland, J., de Courcy, *Ireland and the Irish in Maritime History* (Dublin 1986)

Joyce, P., *Social History of Ancient Ireland* (Dublin 1913)

Knox, H.T., *History of the County Mayo* (Dublin 1908)

Leask, H.G., *Irish Castles and Castellated Houses* (Dundalk 1972)

Loades, D., *The Tudor Court* (London 1992)

McCalmont, R.F., *Memoires of the Binghams* (London 1915)

McClintock, H., *Irish and Highland Dress* (Dundalk 1950)

McClintock, H., *Handbook of the Old Irish Dress* (Dundalk 1958)

McCoy, Hayes, G., *Scots Mercenary Forces in Ireland, 1565-1607* (1937)

Mac Lysaght, E., *Irish Life in the 17th Century* (Cork 1939)

MacCurtain, M., *Tudor and Stuart Ireland* (Dublin 1972)

MacCurtain, M. O'Dowd, M., eds. *Women in Early Modern Ireland* (Dublin 1991)

Mason, T., *The Islands of Ireland* (London 1936)

Maxwell, C., *The Stranger in Ireland* (London 1934)

Moody,T. Martin, F. Byrnes, F., eds. *A New History of Ireland* vol III (Oxford 1976)

Neale, J., *Elizabeth I and her Parliaments, 1584-1601* (London 1958)

Nicholls, K., *Gaelic and Gaelicised Ireland in the Middle Ages* (Dublin 1972)

O'Brien, G., *Economic History of Ireland in the 17th Century* (Dublin 1919)

O'Faolain, S., *The Great O'Neill* (London 1950)

O'Hart, J., *Irish Pedigrees* (New York 1915)

O'Raghallaigh, T., *Filí agus Filídheacht Chonnacht* (Dublin 1938)

Otway, C., *A Tour Of Connaught* (Dublin 1839)

Praeger, R.L., *The Way That I Went* (1937)

Prockter, A. Taylor, R., *The A to Z of Elizabethan London* (London 1979)

Ridley, J., *Henry VIII* (London 1984)

Smith, L.B., *The Elizabethan Epic* (London 1966)

Stanley, J., ed. *Bold in Her Breeches* (London 1995)

Thackeray, W. M., *The Irish Sketch Book* (London 1902)

Thomas, D.A., *The Illustrated Armada Handbook* (London 1988)

Townsend, J.H., *Buccaneer Queen* (1902)

Walsh, M, Kerney., *Destruction by Peace* (Armagh 1986)

Westropp, T., *Clare Island Survey* (Dublin 1911)

Wilson, P., *The Beginnings of Modern Ireland* (Dublin 1912)

## Journals and Articles

*Dublin University Magazine*, vol LIII (1959)

*Folklore*, vol XXVIII no 4

*Galway Archaeological and Historical Society*, vols I-VII1, XVIII

*Irish Genealogist*, vol I

*Irish Sword*, vol I

*Kerry Archaeological Society*, vol VIII (1975)

*Lord Of the Isles Voyage Brochure* (1993)

Nichols, K., *Land, Law and Society in Sixteenth Century Ireland* (Dublin 1976)

O'Morain, P., *Five Hundred Years in the History of Murrisk Abbey* (Mayo News 7 & 14 Sepyember, 1957)

Ordnance Survey. *Letters Relating to the County of Mayo,* vols I, II, ed. John O'Donovan (Dublin 1862)

Ordnance Survey. *Letters relating to the County of Galway* ed. John O'Donovan (Dublin 1862)

*Proceeding of the Royal Irish Academy,* vol 36

*Revue Celtique,* vol XLIX

*Ulster Journal of Archaeology,* vols II, IV, V, VIII

# *Index*